THE
BOOK OF DOUBT

AIDAN DOYLE

Illustrated by Kathleen Jennings

THE MAP OF SUBMISSIONLAND

CONTENTS

THE LONG ROAD

INTRODUCTION

Once you've achieved ultimate success as a writer, you can cross *The Rainbow Bridge of Sparkly Happiness* and take your promised place in *The Citadel of Real Writers*. In this hallowed realm, you will wake up at three o'clock every morning, run an ultramarathon while dictating the edits to your next bestselling book, then partake in a session of extreme yoga until your pores ooze productivity. Every word you write will cause a profound shift in the cultural landscape. Devoted readers will name their WiFi networks after characters from your books. You will never again experience a moment of self-doubt. You will finally be a *Real Writer*.

It's hard to resist the temptation to believe that once you achieve your writing dreams, all of your doubts will go away. What's the point of doing all that hard work to finish a book if it doesn't bring you ultimate happiness?

I've enjoyed writing as long as I can remember. A comment on my school report from when I was ten reads, "I believe that if Aidan was given the opportunity he would spend a large part of each and every day writing stories." In the many years since I've written many short stories and a few novels. By some measures I'm a successful writer. I was professionally published at the age of eighteen and I've had more than 100 short stories and articles published. I've been shortlisted for several awards and I was the youngest writer to receive an entry in *The Encyclopedia of Australian Science Fiction and Fantasy*. By other measures I'm a failure. I've never been close to earning a living as a writer. None of my stories have been published in a year's best collection. I've never had a novel published. Everyone has a different definition of success. You shouldn't listen to people who say you're not a real writer if you don't write every day or you don't earn a living from your writing.

Doubt is a part of every profession, but rejection in an artistic endeavour can have a particularly sharp sting when your creation is so personal. Many writers start out by believing they'll be successful when they get something published. Their first short story is published, but then they keep getting rejection letters. Maybe it was a fluke. True success must be when they get a novel published. Then their novel comes out and it doesn't get much attention. Expectations adjust. There are always goals out of reach and other writers who have achieved more. There's always something new to worry about.

This book began as a blog post I wrote partly out of my frustration at having been a writer for so long and still not having a novel published, and partly due to the level of self-doubt afflicting so many of my writing friends. I was surprised at the attention *The Science Fiction Writer's Hierarchy of Doubt* received. Even Neil Gaiman tweeted a link to it.

I decided to expand the original blog post. I revised the hierarchy and enlisted Kathleen Jennings to provide some illustrations, including *The Map of Submissionland*. As part of the research for this book, I read more than fifty books on motivation, productivity, happiness and confidence. In many cases, the basic message can be boiled down to: *Try to be positive. Believe in yourself. Value relationships and experiences over material possessions. Be grateful for what you have.*

I also learned there are rules for writing this kind of book. You must mention Mihaly Csikszentmihalyi and *flow*. You must include an inspirational quote from Steve Jobs.

Some friends asked me if it's worth reading self-help books. It depends on your own situation and varies by book. The more useful books contain practical information on different ways of improving your life. There can also be value in being reminded of the obvious things. Learning that even bestselling authors experience doubt can be a source of consolation. You're not alone in your struggle.

Happiness is such an important topic, that even if a book is mostly anecdotes and summaries of studies, if there's one piece of advice or wisdom that particularly resonates with you, it can be worth reading. I enjoy reading books about decision making, psychology and behavioral economics. Part of the reason for writing this book was to give myself an excuse to spend time researching these topics. Of course, reading self-help books is the easy part. The real value comes from implementing their suggestions. I experimented with different productivity methods, life hacks, and motivational apps to see which ones worked for me.

It's also worth considering who the audience is for self-help books. Most of the books I read contained no references to the extra difficulties faced by people from marginalized communities. I once took an online course on computer game design and the white male instructor encouraged students to share their work online, adding that the worst thing that could happen was that people didn't like your game design. It can be harder to deal with criticism when it's an attack aimed at your identity. When it comes to writing advice, it's easy to fall into the trap of being too prescriptive. *This worked for me, so you must do it this way.* Most of the productivity advice I read didn't take into account that people with chronic illness may be unable to consistently devote time to tasks.

I wanted provide a wide range of experiences, backgrounds and opinions. The book's twenty-two guest essays are from a diverse range of writers and cover topics such as dealing with doubt, grief, jealousy and failure; the importance of representation in media; and the inevitable struggles that accompany a long writing career.

This isn't a book about the craft of writing. Nor should

this book's advice be a substitute for seeking appropriate treatment for mental health issues. *The Writer's Book of Doubt* is intended as a source of consolation and inspiration. May it serve as a path through *The Forest of Doubt* and *The Mountains of Deadlines*.

DOUBT

THE WRITER'S HIERARCHY OF DOUBT

Why don't I have any ideas?

Why haven't I written anything?

Why haven't I written anything good?

Why won't anyone publish my stories?

Why won't anyone pay me for my stories?

Why won't any of the professional magazines buy my stories?

What if my first professional sale was a fluke?

Why do I need to worry about social media?

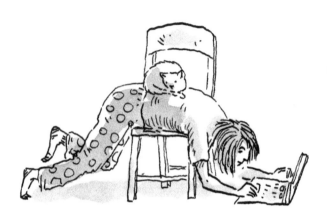

Why do people always get my name wrong?

Why is it so long since I sold a story?

Why won't anyone famous follow me on Twitter?

Why is there never any buzz about any of my stories?

Why aren't I on any recommended reading lists?

Why aren't my stories as good as Ted Chiang's?

Why doesn't anyone remember me when I meet them again at writers' festivals?

Why aren't I getting invited to any secret author parties?

Why aren't I getting asked to contribute to invitation-only anthologies?

Why have all my writing group classmates sold their novels?

Why isn't my name listed on the anthology's front cover?

Why is the photo of my neighbour's cat the most popular thing on my web site?

Why haven't any of my blog posts got me a book deal?

Why aren't I nominated for any awards?

Why don't agents respond to my queries?

Why haven't I won any awards?

Why don't I have an agent?

Why do all my friends expect me to introduce them to my agent?

Why hasn't my agent sold my book?

When are my family going to stop asking me when I'm going to sell a book?

Why did I get such a small advance for my book?

Why does my author photo look so bad?

Why don't I have anything interesting to put in my author bio?

Why did my book get such a bad cover?

Why isn't anyone reviewing my book?

Why did I read the reviews of my book?

Why do all my friends expect me to give them a free copy of my book?

Why doesn't the book store have my book?

Why don't I have a bigger social media platform?

Why isn't anyone buying my book?

Why are people blaming me for the price of the ebook?

Why doesn't the book store have my book in the display window?

Why doesn't anyone want to interview me?

Why did I say that during the interview?

Why does everyone think that just because I've sold a book that I must be rich?

Why isn't anyone pirating my book?

Why isn't my agent answering my emails?

Why aren't I on *The New York Times Best Seller* list?

Why haven't I ever seen anyone reading my book on the plane?

Why did that idiot who can't string two sentences together sell more books than me?

Why do people assume I agree with everything my characters say?

Why hasn't a publisher asked if they could do a collection of my stories?

Why did my editor get a job at a different publisher?

Why aren't I getting invited to any writers' festivals?

Why isn't my book being translated into more languages?

Why aren't my stories as good as Ted Chiang's?

Why isn't anyone making fan art based on my stories?

Why are fan fiction writers making my characters do terrible things?

Why do my fans expect me to be as exciting as my main character?

How am I ever going to follow up on my first book with anything as good?

Why can't I make a living from my novels?

Why doesn't the publisher want my next book?

Why hasn't anyone made a movie or TV series based on my books?

Why does Tom Cruise want to play the lead role in the movie based on my book?

Why doesn't anyone understand how long it takes to write a book?

Why isn't anyone accusing me of corrupting today's youth?

Why isn't anyone naming their children after my characters?

Why doesn't anyone want to visit the bar I used to drink at?

Why don't any museums want a copy of the first draft of my novel?

Why does everyone say they like my earlier work better?

Why does that Russian literature professor think my books are too long?

Why doesn't my former university want to put a statue of me in their courtyard?

Why isn't the religion I started as profitable as Scientology?

Why haven't I won the Nobel Prize for Literature?

Why hasn't anyone named an asteroid after me?

Why haven't I been chosen as Earth's representative for the Galactic Senate?

Why aren't my stories as good as Ted Chiang's?

DON'T SELF-REJECT! #dontselfreject

R. Lemberg

R. (Rose) Lemberg is a queer, bigender immigrant from Eastern Europe and Israel. Their fiction and poetry have appeared in Light-speed's Queer Destroy Science Fiction, Beneath Ceaseless Skies, Uncanny, and many other venues. R's work has been a finalist for the Nebula, Crawford, and other awards. Their novella The Four Profound Weaves is forthcoming from Tachyon Press. You can find more of their work on their Patreon: patreon.com/roselemberg

An earlier version of this essay was published on Patreon.

For emerging marginalized writers, lack of information, lack of mentoring and self-rejection are familiar and painful. Nisi Shawl's important and powerful essay "Unqualified" in *Cascadia Subduction Zone* made me think yet again about what I can personally do to make the field more welcoming. I often think about it, and do the best I can to practice what I preach.

New marginalized writers often do not have the same kind of access to a network of mentors, supporters, and information which is available to less marginalized people. I often hear from marginalized creators who are discouraged by clueless and antagonistic critiques, hurt by badly phrased rejections for #ownvoices stories. We often come into the field with pre-existing hurts; many of us have been told—years before we started sending our work out—that we are not good enough. Our experiences have been invalidated and our self-confidence rattled before we even send out that first submission.

Self-rejection is a huge issue for marginalized people, myself included—self-rejection not just from sending out completed work, but from writing itself, from creating, and from finishing projects. Many of us fear that what we have to say is hopeless/irrelevant/not good enough for markets; many of us feel that we must endlessly perfect a piece of work before anybody can see it. These feelings are familiar to emerging creators, but also to professionally published marginalized creators. It is easy to envision the most painful scenarios because we have been hurt and hurt before.

What is the point of even trying? I hear these fears from so many brilliant people who are afraid to finish stories and poems, who fear that their window of opportunity to become successful is fleeting, who fear that "diversity slots" have already been taken by other writers, who see #ownvoices work rejected over and over while non-#ownvoices work gets the spotlight, who worry that marginalized creators are always expected to write only one kind of story.

In this, I feel that our people are especially harmed by the "rapid, youthful success" paradigm that is so pervasive in our field, and in other creative fields. You internalize that you have to "make it" (whatever that means) by 20, 25, certainly by 30; sure, there are exceptions, but marginalized people often begin to feel that they've "fallen behind" already in their twenties.

But if you are marginalized in any way, you all too often work—and emerge—more slowly than you would like, because there are institutional obstacles to overcome, because you are struggling to survive in a hostile world, because you may be trying to work through traumas, to find community and support, to gain access to information. All too often you also need to push against the painful and harmful misconceptions—both external and internalized —of what your work should look like. Once you do that, once you begin telling your own stories, the field may be even less receptive to your work.

The life of a marginalized writer all too often involves the feelings of anguish, frustration, and fear—and creative writing it's not the most mental-health-friendly pursuit to begin with!

What I offer marginalized writers is a hashtag and a sentence:

Don't self-reject.

Marginalized writers, please don't self-reject from writing. We need your voices desperately. We need each other's voices.

Marginalized writers, #dontselfreject from sending work out. Please, send it out. Please, let it sit there in slush piles; and while the work sits there, please #dontselfreject from writing new material and please #dontselfreject from sending that out as well.

Marginalized writers, #dontselfreject from querying magazine editors if you have questions, or if you did not get a response. Work might be misplaced or lost.

If you have work that doesn't fit the guidelines only slightly, and you would not dream of querying an editor, please understand this: as an editor, I received more queries from white Anglo men than I did from any other demographic. Marginalized creators are much less likely to query an editor. But if you query, you might get a positive answer.

As an editor, I noticed that where a non-marginalized person sends out a good-enough story, a marginalized person agonizes endlessly until they deem their work "perfect" (often a moving target). Editors may solicit, encourage, and even cajole, and marginalized writers still often feel trepidation, still often feel that the solicited work is not good enough to send. I see this over and over—in numbers, in conversations, I see it in the way our people talk themselves down. Please don't self-reject.

Create it. Send it out. Create more.

It is hard. It is painful. It is scary. Acceptance is never guaranteed and might be harder to obtain. But—we need your voices. We need our own voices. Don't self-reject.

We should not downplay just how difficult this is. Just how excruciating. How discouraging. How lonely. So if you feel you can reach out to someone else with words of encouragement, that helps. Let us support each other to create, to send out, to revise, to try again, and not to despair, because our work is worth the work.

This is my message to you as an editor, as a writer, as a multiply marginalized person who fights self-rejection every day.

Thank you for reading this. Thank you for surviving. Thank you for your voice. And please #dontselfreject.

THE AWESOMENESS DOSSIER

Someone at my new job described me as a 'human Pinterest board' the other day and I saved that to my special folder of strange compliments I want to remember forever.
  - Laurie Penny

The Awesomeness Dossier is a folder with clear plastic sheets in which I put printouts of things which make me happy about my writing. Positive reviews of my stories. Illustrations that have accompanied my stories. My award nomination announcements. Kind things people have said about my writing on Twitter. Particularly enthusiastic comments from someone critiquing one of my stories. If I get a rejection which particularly stings, the folder is visible proof that my writing doesn't always suck. I highly recommend creating your own Awesomeness Dossier.

It doesn't have to be only related to writing. You can include photos of friends and family and happy events. Or favorite cute animal photos. Happiness researcher Sonja Lyubomirsky talks about how she created a savoring album which she takes with her when she travels. "Whenever I travel for business, even for a day, I carry a little photo album that has pictures of my kids at different ages... I look at it a lot—in planes, hotel rooms, and the audience of conference talks—and it never fails to give me a happiness boost. You can create such a savoring/memory album yourself. It can have photos of your favorite people, places, or things—family, friends, pets, famous paintings, etc... Or it can have other happy-inducing or meaningful items— your acceptance letter to college, a love note, a favorite recipe, a niece's drawing, or an article about your favorite actor. Look at this album on a regular basis but not too often, so as to stave off adaptation to its pleasure. You don't want the same thing to happen to the items in your savoring album as might happen to a special photo on your nightstand or computer screen; when it's up for a long enough time, you fail to notice it altogether. This savoring album is essentially a strategy to create and savor the memories (the mental photographs) of your positive experiences. It's also valuable to review the album in less happy times, when you're especially needful of a boost."

Writer Jennika Baines uses a similar technique for her email. "At a former colleague's suggestion I have an email folder just called *Happy* where I file emails in which someone says something kind or says thank you or says something else that makes me happy to read. If you don't have one, give yourself the gift of a Happy folder."

THE LITERAL SEAT OF MY PANTS

Crystal M. Huff

Crystal Huff (pronouns: they/them) is the Executive Director of Include Better. Crystal has a long history in tech and geek culture, and is committed to anti-harassment and impostor syndrome work. They have been an invited speaker in Sweden, Finland, China, Iceland, Israel, Canada, UK, and across the USA. Over 2,000 people world-wide have taken Crystal's impostor syndrome workshops.

Crystal speaks fluent English, rusty American Sign Language, and beginner Finnish cussing. They are an editor of translations for the Future Affairs Administration in Beijing and associate editor for Resist Fascism (2018).

> *Impostor Syndrome: The feeling that you aren't really qualified for the work you're doing or aren't really deserving of the successes you've achieved, and will be discovered as a fraud. Many women, People of Color, QUILTBAG persons, and others experience this, especially when they've (we've) been socialized to value others' opinions of work above their (our) own. Want help overcoming your impostor syndrome and/or decreasing its incidence in your community? This practical three-hour workshop provides key takeaways, tools, and advice, delivered with a good dose of humor.*

With this paragraph I pitch my favorite gig, professionally speaking: my impostor syndrome workshop.

I'm going to tell you a story that I have never before written down, about one of my own experiences of impostor syndrome. Imagine me turning the brightest shade of red possible while typing these words. Think, more like a ripe tomato than a pale pink rose.

A couple of years ago, I was invited to give the afore-mentioned recently-developed three-hour workshop on impostor syndrome at a prominent university. I was incredibly excited. A connection via a friend had landed me this plum opportunity, and it was my first chance to give the workshop in an academic setting.

I did several of the usual things you might imagine someone in my shoes doing, particularly someone who had been raised as a girl. I bought makeup and took a YouTube crash course on applying it. I styled my hair in a way I was told complemented the shape of my face. I bought swishy new black pants and shiny new shoes.

On the day of the workshop, I looked damn sharp.

I arrived early, as I always try to do, and went about setting up the room.

Workshop participants started to arrive, as did my friend who worked for the university. The time to begin the workshop drew nigh, so I stepped up to the speaker platform, toward the podium where my materials lay.

On the last step up, I managed to step on the hem of my swishy new pants. To my immense and undying horror, I literally managed to pants myself. I'm rather confident I displayed my underwear before I managed to catch my clothing as it fell toward the floor.

Less than five minutes remained before the appointed hour of the workshop. I wouldn't say the room was full, but certainly I sensed all eyes upon me. I needed to recover, fast!

My friend instantly became the best rodeo clown I have ever seen, and distracted the students in the room by making sure everyone had a writing utensil and a copy of the workshop handout. I used that moment to pull my pants back up, but my dignity remained somewhere below my ankles, emotionally speaking. Dropping trousers in public reads as the opposite of professionalism, no matter how you look at it, and I had been so desperate to be a professional in this setting. Instead, I felt like a fraud and a failure.

In every impostor syndrome workshop, I teach people that there are ways we can inoculate ourselves against the onslaught of impostor syndrome feelings, and I give some options for how to avoid spinning our wheels when we start having difficulty. For example, I suggest everyone keep a folder of compliments they've received from people they trust to be honest, in order to remind them of successes they've had in the past. I tell workshop participants to think of their proudest, happiest, shiniest moment and try to recapture the glow of that moment – reverse the emotional flow when they might otherwise spiraling into feeling like a fraud. I advocate for compiling a record of projects that one is working on and periodic progress updates, so it's easier to see the advances made over time. (Aidan Doyle tells me he maintains an "Awesomeness Dossier," and I am completely going to steal this title for future use!) Such records can help us recognize that mistakes are part of the process of developing skills, even skills we may take for granted later on. Reviewing these records during a challenging period can be a powerful way to prove to oneself that it's possible to achieve a goal despite setbacks and doubts.

I additionally teach participants in my workshops that it can be helpful to recall some of the societal factors that have contributed to their feelings of fraud. Research indicates that acknowledging these factors explicitly can help in overcoming them, and that conclusion has certainly been supported by anecdotal data from my work. Many people who suffer from impostor syndrome do so in part because of social conditioning, having received implicit and explicit messages that they are frauds or doomed to fail. Stereotype threat can be a notable factor for impostor syndrome sufferers marginalized by society. Naming these issues can return power to the individual confronting them and deepen someone's self-compassion, which can be a turning point in combatting factors of impostor syndrome.

Before my fateful, lowered-pants day, I knew that putting these methods into practice isn't as easy as talking about them, but "dropping trou" in public was a whole new level of education on the matter. I'd like to say that I took some deep, calming breaths and chose an appropriate method to address my feelings. The reality of the situation looked a bit more like me quietly hyperventilating while I dug in my pockets for my phone. If I recall correctly, I was reminding myself over and over that I do this for a LIVING and this will be a GREAT STORY someday if I can JUST SURVIVE THE NEXT THREE HOURS.

When my phone finally emerged, however, I discovered something magical had occurred.

While I'd been panicking on stage, my beloved spouse and my housemate had been chatting away in our household chat app. My housemate was enthusiastically talking about how their latest job interview had gone—this might be a perfect new position for them. My spouse was offering hearty congratulations, and delivering the good news that he'd received a raise at work. There were many high fives and hugs in text, all around.

This chat log had an instant positive impact on my emotions and outlook. It was a strong reminder that there was a part of my life going well regardless of what kind of day I was having, professionally. Witnessing the support and cheer of those two, both so important to me in a very different aspect of my life, was enough to brighten up my mental landscape despite my predicament. I took another breath, checked the time, and announced to the room that we'd begin shortly.

The group chat I encountered in that instant was the result of serendipity. I certainly couldn't count on my spouse getting a raise every time I felt overwhelmed! The key, though, was the reminder of my life as a multi-faceted effort; I was reassured that no matter what happened at work, it would not change how my loved ones felt about me. As a human being, I was more than any particular embarrassing experience I had, even one as excruciating as this.

I've thought quite a bit about this event in the years since then. What else could I have done, in the moment? I talk with folks in my workshops about keeping some quick, essential "pick-me-ups" on hand—happy-making things that are in some way sensory or even visceral, to help direct our thoughts and feelings in a more productive direction. I have a friend who carries a smooth stone in her pocket, a reminder of the beach where she got married. A former colleague told me he put a picture of his grandparents in his wallet. The smell of leather and the smiles on their faces are very evocative for him. For me, it's a folder on my phone full of friends' baby photos and silly internet memes, the kind that make me laugh out loud.

The mementos we carry with us through life can have a huge impact on our emotional well-being. These items may be only of temporary comfort, but sometimes we need to get through the moment in order to arrive in a better frame of mind in the future, and positive impact can be just as cumulative as negative.

In terms of the longer-term outlook, there are some deeper introspections one can do to combat impostor syndrome. Something else that I carry in my phone is an exercise I did a few years ago with a close friend. We each spent a few minutes making lists in our notebooks—"What Makes Me Awesome" and "What Makes You Awesome." Writing about my friend's superlative characteristics was easy! And writing what I admired in myself was hard! My friend felt the same way, though, and they helped me see myself differently: "You are awesome because you learn how to say thank you wherever you go in the world." I cherish what they wrote, in part because I never would have noticed or valued this aspect of myself if not for their words.

Perspective from others who suffer from impostor syndrome, even strangers, can also provide aid and solace in this struggle. For example, I have long admired Maya Angelou, the celebrated Black American poet, singer, and activist who received countless honorary degrees, three Grammy Awards, a Pulitzer Prize nomination, and the National Medal of Arts. Angelou, too, appears to have suffered from impostor syndrome. Before her death in 2014, she wrote, "*I have written 11 books, but each time I think, 'Uh oh, they're going to find out now. I've run a game on everybody, and they're going to find me out.'*" I take comfort in the fact that Maya Angelou shared my struggle, and I appreciate that she spoke publicly about it. I feel that Angelou did an amazing job of leading by example; I strive to be more like her in this.

Going back to the day in question, eventually my pants-defying impostor syndrome workshop drew to a close. After the last student exited the room, I girded my loins, so to speak, and walked over toward my friend to begin an Awkward Conversation.

"Thank you for distracting everyone when I tripped," I said (and yes, I was the color of a ripe tomato then, too). "So, uh, not to be weird or anything, but … could people see the color of my underwear? I just need to know how bad it was."

"Oh!" My rodeo clown friend looked over at me. "I'd forgotten that happened!"

I will never forget the indignity of dropping my pants in public, dear reader. I can't. But I will also remember that the day concluded with this perfect moment, a reminder that what's going on for me, psychologically, is far less likely to be noticed or recalled by others. When I'm feeling like an impostor, it's really hard to put workshop exercises into practice, but I try to remember that I can pull through, and have done so successfully in the past. That helps me feel like a pro, in fact. I hope that reading this story helps you, too.

WHY DOESN'T MY DOPPELGANGER HAVE IMPOSTOR SYNDROME?

My grandma used to say, 'Never let self-doubt drive your car. It rides in the back seat.'
 - *Mindy Halleck*

15 books on shelves, 10 more under contract, I still spend at least 1 hour a day convinced I'm never going to 'make it' in case you were wondering if THAT feeling ever goes away.
 - *Victoria Schwab*

Embrace impostor syndrome. Revel in the fact you have fooled every-one. You are a Trickster Goddess. You are the Impostor Child for Deception and Clever Ruses.
 - *Eli Barraza*

Neil Gaiman has written about the time he met Neil Armstrong, who said he felt out of place amongst all the talented people. "And then he pointed to the hall of people, and said words to the effect of, 'I just look at all these people, and I think, what the heck am I doing here? They've made amazing things. I just went where I was sent.' And I said, 'Yes. But you were the first man on the moon. I think that counts for something.' And I felt a bit better. Because if Neil Armstrong felt like an impostor, maybe everyone did. Maybe there weren't any grown-ups, only people who had worked hard and also got lucky and were slightly out of their depth, all of us doing the best job we could, which is all we can really hope for."

Impostor syndrome affects some of the most powerful

people in the world. People who seem like they are full of confidence. Michelle Obama told students that "I still have a little [bit of] impostor syndrome... It doesn't go away, that feeling that you shouldn't take me that seriously. What do I know? I share that with you because we all have doubts in our abilities, about our power and what that power is."

I'm an outlier in that I've never really experienced impostor syndrome as a writer. Ever since primary (elementary) school, I've thought of myself as someone good at making up stories. That feeling's never gone away. When it comes to computer programming though, I've sometimes wondered why anyone would give me a job when clearly I don't know what I'm doing. I'm not sure why I've been immune to impostor syndrome when it comes to writing. Perhaps it's because the encouragement I received as a child helped cement my identity as a story maker. The difference when it comes to computer programming is that I feel vulnerable when I don't think I know enough about the topic. Technology is always changing and I feel like I don't do enough to keep up with all the new programming languages and frameworks.

It's easy to fall into the trap of believing impostor syndrome will go away once you reach a certain level of success. Once I get a book published, I'll feel like a real writer. Once I win an award, I'll be full of confidence. That doesn't often happen. In fact, achievement can actually make it worse. Success can push you into new situations—being asked to make presentations, being invited to contribute to anthologies—that you feel you're not qualified for. Your work and your failures will also be more visible. If your first book wins awards, this can place tremendous pressure on you when it comes to your next book. Being given the opportunity to fail safely when you're younger is one way that can show you that failure isn't always awful. It teaches you how to manage failure and its consequences. Part of this also revolves around who is given the privilege of being able to fail without harsh judgment.

In her TED Talk, researcher Carol Dweck mentions a Chicago school where students who didn't reach the passing grade were instead given a grade, *Not Yet*. She says, "And I thought that was fantastic, because if you get a failing grade, you think, I'm nothing, I'm nowhere. But if you get the grade *Not Yet* you understand that you're on a learning curve. It gives you a path into the future."

It's easy to fall into the trap of believing that everyone is enjoying more success than you. Writers who've never been published may think you're living the dream because you've had a book published. Whereas you're comparing yourself to your friends on the bestseller lists. It's not easy, but try to put things into perspective.

So how do you reduce impostor syndrome? Keeping track of your accomplishments via an *Awesomeness Dossier* is an easy method to implement. The idea of *faking it till you make it*, is another way. If you fool yourself into believing that you deserve to be on that writing panel it can help reduce your anxiety.

Talking with other writers can decrease your sense of isolation. Learning that more successful writers struggle with impostor syndrome can be both encouraging and discouraging.

When it comes to computer programming, I know that no one can possibly keep up with all of the changes in technology. It's not the worst thing in the world to admit you don't know something.

THE MEDIOCRE WHITE MAN CONFIDENCE
FACTORY

Thank you to the person who taught me the phrase 'I'm sorry but I haven't budgeted for any more unpaid work this month.'
- Kerry Hudson

One of the things that surprised me when I attended the Clarion South writing workshop was how many of the other students said that applying to the workshop had made them anxious. It was the second time I'd applied. The first time I'd been rejected and that had disappointed me, but it didn't make me feel anxious. I just assumed the writers who were accepted instead of me had things the workshop organizers were looking for, and it didn't necessarily reflect on my abilities as a writer. I applied again and this time I was accepted. Although I get disappointed with rejections, I'm lucky that I've never doubted I was a *real* writer. Part of this is due to how men are treated by society.

There's a much referenced Hewlett-Packard internal report from the 1980s that showed that men applied for promotions when they met at least sixty percent of the job requirements. Women applied for a promotion when they met one hundred percent of the requirements.

Writers Katty Kay and Claire Shipman talk about how playing team sports can develop confidence and boys are more likely to continue to play team sports. "Girls who play team sports are more likely to graduate from college, find a job, and be employed in male-dominated industries. There's even a direct link between playing sports in high school and earning a bigger salary as an adult. Learning to own victory and survive defeat in sports is apparently good training for owning triumphs and surviving setbacks at work."

Kay and Shipman mention research conducted by Zachary Estes who tested students on spatial puzzles. The men performed better, but when Estes looked more closely at the results he found the women hadn't done as well because they hadn't tried to solve some of the puzzles. He repeated the experiment, this time telling students they had to try to solve all the puzzles. This time the women performed as well as the men.

This shouldn't be interpreted as a criticism of women for not being confident enough. It's a recognition of how society enforces gender roles. Women are more likely to have their competency challenged by others. When computer scientist Katie Bouman was announced as the person responsible for the algorithm which helped create the first image of a black hole, some people didn't want to acknowledge that a woman could play such a pivotal role. Her *Wikipedia* entry was even flagged as *not notable* by someone who suggested her accomplishments didn't mean she deserved her own page. There are plenty of examples of how male and female fictional heroes are treated differently. *Luke Skywalker is a real Jedi. Rey is a Mary Sue who hasn't earned her powers.*

Not only do you have to worry about being confident, you need to insulate yourself from the attacks. White is so often taken as the default in many English speaking countries that if you focus on characters from other backgrounds you're *being political*. If you're transgender or genderqueer the attacks can be even worse. Although social media can expose you to hate, it also makes it easier to find role models, mentors and peers. Build a support network of fellow writers. Listen to people like Anita Sarkeesian and N.K. Jemisin talk about how they handle the attacks.

The situation is even more complicated when it comes to applying for story submission calls targeted at particular demographics. The editors want to encourage marginalized writers, but that might involve publicly outing part of your identity. There was a recent instance of an agent rejecting a bisexual writer because they *weren't gay enough*.

I have sleep apnea and that might qualify me to submit to a call for disabled writers. But am I disabled enough? I don't think of myself as disabled and my condition has little impact on my daily life. If I had a story accepted, would I be stealing a place from someone who was really disabled? If you were born in Australia and have one parent from China, do you qualify for a grant aimed at Asian writers? Again, this is part of a systemic problem—if there were more opportunities for writers from marginalized communities there wouldn't be as much pressure to self-label when it came to submitting stories. There wouldn't be the problem of thinking you were taking a place from someone more deserving. How you handle these questions is a deeply personal issue. Many editors don't want you to self-reject. If you identify as belonging to the community, they want to read your stories. Read the essays from writers published in projects like *Disabled People Destroy Science Fiction* or *People of Colo(u)r Destroy Science Fiction* and see how they grappled with these issues.

Some writers have argued that placing too much emphasis on self-esteem makes people less able to cope with the inevitable setbacks they'll encounter. How do you make yourself more confident without acting like an annoying loudmouth? Part of it involves believing in your own competence without denigrating others. Curiosity is a way of keeping yourself humble. It involves admitting that you don't know everything.

If you act like you know what you're doing, most people will assume you know what you're doing. Submit stories to magazines. Don't immediately disqualify yourself from talking on that panel. If you think a writing workshop will be beneficial for you, apply for it.

Amy Cuddy did a popular TED talk and book on her research into how power poses (standing like Wonder Woman—hands on hip and chin up) can increase confidence. Follow up studies failed to reproduce her results and although Cuddy published a response to her detractors, the evidence is at best mixed. There's always the placebo effect though and if power posing makes you feel more confident, there can still be value in it.

An alternative path is to focus more on dealing with your self-doubt than trying to gain more confidence. Writer Tara Mohr suggests trying to identify when your inner critic is talking and giving your critic a name. "Create a character that symbolizes the voice of fear within you... Pick a character that illustrates how the voice of fear feels in you, and name your character. When you hear the voice of fear, greet it: 'Oh, Cruella, I see you've come to visit. Hello.' Why does this work? Creating a character helps you separate the real you from the part of you that's afraid. Your fears come from that instinctual part of the brain that seeks to avoid risk at any cost-not from your core self, your inner wisdom, or your dreams. Naming the voice of fear, visualizing it as a character and observing it helps you get back in charge."

There's also the idea of cosplaying a successful writer. In an article *Building the Story of Ourselves,* Kameron Hurley writes about trying to be more confident at a convention, "When I'm on a panel, or at the bar, or in conversation, and I'm stuck for what to say, I think, 'What would a famous author do?' and the answer is a famous author would be totally confident, would be generous and interested in asking people questions, would be gregarious and tell jokes and ask people about their work and just generally have a great, confident, easy-going time, because hey, they are famous and successful and have no cares in the world. Weirdly, this *cosplaying a famous writer* thing works for me. I tell myself a story. I play the part. I do know that this 'fake it 'til you make it' mentality is easier for privileged people, for sure. It's much easier for, say, white men who've been told their whole lives that they are special, by culture and by media, to fake this. That doesn't mean the rest of us can't do it."

UPGRADING YOUR ARMOR CLASS

So much of my work as a teacher and mentor involves telling writers not to worry about things. Learning not to worry too much is crucial, not only because we have very little control over the book after it leaves our hands but also because this kind of worry is toxic to creativity.
  - Lan Samantha Chang

I want to be in the arena. I want to be brave with my life. And when we make the choice to dare greatly, we sign up to get our asses kicked. We can choose courage or we can choose comfort, but we can't have both. Not at the same time... A lot of cheap seats in the arena are filled with people who never venture onto the floor. They just hurl mean-spirited criticisms and put-downs from a safe distance. The problem is, when we stop caring what people think and stop feeling hurt by cruelty, we lose our ability to connect. But when we're defined by what people think, we lose the courage to be vulnerable. Therefore, we need to be selective about the feedback we let into our lives. For me, if you're not in the arena also getting your ass kicked, I'm not interested in your feedback.
  - Brené Brown

Most jobs require resilience. If you've worked in customer service, you know how exhausting people can be. Writing teachers often say that it's not the most talented students who ultimately succeed, it's the most persistent. The ones who don't give up after the first few rejections. How do you use vulnerability to make your stories richer yet remain resilient in the face of what can feel like personal attacks?

In *Daring Greatly*, shame researcher Brené Brown writes about how making yourself vulnerable can be important for creativity. "Vulnerability is not knowing victory or defeat, it's understanding the necessity of both; it's engaging. It's being all in. Vulnerability is not weakness, and the uncertainty, risk, and emotional exposure we face every day are not optional. Our only choice is a question of engagement. Our willingness to own and engage with our vulnerability determines the depth of our courage and the clarity of our purpose; the level to which we protect ourselves from being vulnerable is a measure of our fear and disconnection."

It's important to separate your sense of self-worth from the things you make. Brown writes, "Sharing something that you've created is a vulnerable but essential part of engaged and wholehearted living. It's the epitome of daring greatly. But because of how you were raised or how you approach the world, you've knowingly or unknowingly attached your self-worth to how your product or art is received. In simple terms, if they love it, you're worthy; if they don't, you're worthless." This often stops people from sharing their work. Or they share it and are crushed when the work is rejected. She says that if you tie your self-worth to your work and it succeeds, then this can be worse in the long run for your self-esteem. "Everything shame needs to hijack and control your life is in place. You've handed over your self-worth to what people think. It's panned out a couple of times, but now it feels a lot like Hotel California: You can check in, but you can never leave. You're officially a prisoner of 'pleasing, performing, and perfecting.'"

Particularly when it comes to movements like #OwnVoices, writing can make you feel vulnerable. How do you separate your self-worth from your work when people criticize elements of the story tied to your identity? Marginalized writers can receive particularly awful comments. Your critique group tell you there's no reason to mention the character's sexuality. You write something based on your personal experience and reviewers complain the main character is unlikable and deserved what happened to them. Editors tell you the portrayal of your home country didn't feel believable and the characters' dialog was too sophisticated to be realistic. You shouldn't feel obligated to change your story in response to these prejudiced comments. You might also get comments asking you to explain more about your setting. How much you stop and explain things for people who aren't familiar with your culture is a personal choice.

There's also the pressure you place on yourself when it comes to labeling. *Am I really disabled enough for this to be an #OwnVoices story? If I write a positive portrayal of my culture, I'm ignoring the problems. If I write a negative portrayal, I'm a self-hater who has betrayed my people.*

Being vulnerable needs to be balanced with self-care, especially if you're making yourself vulnerable online. It's good to challenge yourself, but your mental health and safety are of paramount importance.

If you're making yourself more vulnerable, you want to be resilient enough to handle the rejection, setbacks, disappointment and criticism that come your way. Everyone gets rejected. It's an unavoidable part of being a writer. Brown says that being aware of your shame and how it affects you is one of the key things that can help you become more resilient. Sharing your problems and taking solidarity that you aren't the only one experiencing these issues can help make your problems more manageable.

In *21 Days to Resilience*, Zelana Montminy writes that "Being resilient does not mean that you won't encounter problems or have difficulties overcoming a challenge in your life. The difference is that resilient people don't let their adversity define them. At its core, resilience is about being capable and strong enough to persevere in adverse or stressful conditions—and to take away positive meaning from that experience... Lasting happiness requires building upon your strengths, persevering, and being gracious with yourself and others—it's really not about personal achievements or experiencing fleeting positive thoughts and feelings."

Michael Ungar from The Resilience Research Center at Dalhousie University says the resources made available to individuals are often more important than the individual's ability to overcome problems. He conducted a study of at-risk youth and claims his results show "with certainty that resilience depends more on what we receive than what we have within us. These resources, more than individual talent or positive attitude, accounted for the difference between youths who did well and those who slid into drug addiction, truancy and high-risk sexual activity... The science of resilience is clear: The social, political and natural environments in which we live are far more important to our health, fitness, finances and time management than our individual thoughts, feelings or behaviours. When it comes to maintaining well-being and finding success, environments matter. In fact, they may matter just as much, and likely much more, than individual thoughts, feelings or behaviors."

This is another indication that one of the best ways to help yourself is to do your best to help make society fairer.

Finding humor in dark situations is another way to cope. Viktor Frankl wrote about how humor helped him survive a Nazi concentration camp. "Humor was another of the soul's weapons in the fight for self-preservation. It is well known that humor, more than anything else in the human makeup, can afford an aloofness and an ability to rise above any situation, even if only for a few seconds."

How much of your own experiences you choose to share in your writing, is of course a personal decision, but stories with a strong emotional core are often the ones which readers respond the most to. That doesn't mean you have to reproduce a list of all the things that have happened to you, but writing about what scares you the most can give your stories extra resonance. My most reprinted story, *Hokkaido Green* is about a man who feels life has passed him by. The balance between work and experience is something which weighs on me a lot. In some ways this is ridiculous, I've spent years traveling around the world and have visited more than 100 countries. It's not as though I haven't pursued my dreams. But sometimes it feels as though I could have done more with my talent. I was professionally published when I was eighteen. If I'd worked harder, I could have had a few novels published by now. What have I been doing all those years? My fear of letting things slip away is part of what makes this story one of my favorites.

Ultimately you need to be kind to yourself and recognize there's always more you could have done. Find a group of friends who can empathize with your struggles. Rejoice in your achievements and try to take joy from the writing process itself.

HOW TO MEASURE YOUR SENSE OF SELF-WORTH BY YOUR PRODUCTIVITY

We have become a civilization based on work—not even 'productive work' but work as an end and meaning in itself. We have come to believe that men and women who do not work harder than they wish at jobs they do not particularly enjoy are bad people unworthy of love, care, or assistance from their communities.

- David Graeber

How to know you've internalized capitalism: You determine your worth based on your productivity. You feel guilty for resting. Your primary concern is to make yourself profitable. You neglect your health. You think 'hard work' is what brings happiness.

- @_r0sewater

I 100% understand how the dream of being a bestseller, etc… is fuel, but it shouldn't be the reason propelling your craft. If you think you deserve all those things, AWESOME. A touch of self-aware narcissism can be damn good armor considering how soul-scraping this journey is. But I hope you write not for the promise of bright lights, but because your story illuminates a corner of your soul. I hope you trust your voice more than you trust your critics and nay-sayers. I hope you remember that the scaffolding of joy is oftentimes shadows and doubt, and that's okay.

- Roshani Chokshi

If you start thinking that only your biggest and shiniest moments count, you're setting yourself up to feel like a failure most of the time. Personally, I'd rather feel good most of the time, so to me everything counts: the small moments, the medium ones, the successes that make the papers and also the ones that no one knows about but me. The challenge is avoiding being derailed by the big, shiny moments that turn other people's heads.

- Chris Hadfield

A quick online search reveals dozens of blog posts advising you not to link your self-worth to your productivity. Few of these posts have much advice beyond *don't do it*. It's especially hard to stop when society constantly celebrates people for what they produce. If everyone talks about the award winners, it's easy to conclude you're a failure if you're not an award winner. Every year there are lists of the world's richest people. It's rare to see lists of the world's highest tax-payers.

We focus so much attention on the *winners*. Even an achievement like winning an Olympic silver medal can make people feel miserable if they thought they were going to win gold. Bronze medal winners are often happier than silver medalists because they're happy to get a medal, rather than thinking about the gold medal they missed out on. The problem with linking your self-worth to your work is that when failure inevitably comes, it's going to hit you particularly hard and make it harder to keep writing. The desire to succeed at all costs encourages some people to do things they shouldn't. Writers who feel compelled to resort to plagiarism in an effort to get ahead. Writers who are taken advantage of by scam agents and vanity publishers because they're desperate to be published.

It's a problem most people never entirely solve. Taking pride in your work means pain when your work's rejected. You can take steps to ease that pain though. Practice self-compassion and try not to criticize yourself when you don't meet your goals. It's often easier to be kinder to others than to yourself. If missing productivity goals is causing you stress, imagine what you'd say to a friend experiencing the same problem, and direct that kindness at yourself. Take a break from writing and focus on your other interests. When you start writing again, set the smallest possible goal—a sentence a day.

Even when you've got deadlines, it's important to schedule time for play. It will make you more productive and reduce the chance for burnout.

Beware of people who proclaim that writers are better than everyone else. Becoming a writer doesn't necessarily make you a better person. Read interviews with famous writers who say that although writing brought them happiness, it's their family and friends that make them happiest. Don't be the kind of writer who uses their writing as an excuse to avoid your responsibilities.

Being able to laugh at yourself makes things easier. Try not to take yourself too seriously.

And as usual, one of the best ways to make yourself feel better is to help others.

Commiserate with writing friends who support you. They can help you be kind to yourself. However, sometimes having writer friends can upset you if they're more successful. It can make you feel awful when you meet a writing friend you haven't seen for a while and they enthusiastically ask what you've been working on and you've got nothing. Make sure you have friends you can hang out with who aren't going to ask you how your writing is going.

Sometimes people will tell you that writing is a waste of time and you should focus your efforts on a more *productive* career. This can be especially hurtful if family members tell you this. *When are you going to get a real job?* Some people think you're wasting your time unless your writing is bringing in lots of money. Do your best to ignore these comments.

Everyone writes at a different speed. Try not to

compare yourself to writers who produce 23,000 words before breakfast. Prolific writer Seanan McGuire says (in a non-boastful way) that she doesn't post her daily word counts online because she doesn't want beginning writers to compare themselves to her. If you suffer from chronic illness, it can be distressing to compare your current productivity to what you used to be able to achieve. Try not to be hard on yourself.

Sometimes you've been productive but your work is invisible to others because it hasn't been published. You've been working on a mammoth fantasy epic for the last couple of years and people keep asking you when you're going to have more short stories coming out. Or you've written a dozen short stories but haven't been able to sell any of them. These things happen. It can feel like people will forget about you if you don't have a new trilogy coming out every week. Proceed at your own pace.

You don't have to love the writing process all the time. It can be painful and hard work and tiring and disappointing. But it helps if you can celebrate the joy of having made something and keep that separate from what others think of it. Take pleasure from the act of creating a story. I've written half a dozen novels, none of which have been published. Even if I didn't think of them as a learning process, they wouldn't be a waste of time. I derived happiness from the act of making them.

Rewards can motivate you to continue your progress, but when the reward stops, people can lose interest. There have been studies where children were encouraged to use crayons to draw pictures. One group of children were given rewards for their drawings. The other group (in another location) didn't receive any reward. Researchers followed up later on and found that the children who hadn't been given the reward were more likely to still be using the crayons. In *Better Than Before*, Gretchen Rubin writes about her daughter. "If I tell Eliza that she can watch an hour of TV if she reads for an hour, I don't build her habit of reading; I teach her that watching TV is more fun than reading." She compares this to a company which has an employee gym and people who use "the gym for a certain number of times a year gets next year's membership for free." The reward for exercise is more exercise, which encourages you to view it as a worthwhile activity in of itself.

Celebrating the small things can help you avoid putting your happiness on hold until you achieve your major goals. Try to find pleasure in indulging your senses. I get deliriously excited about donuts and cakes.

In *The How of Happiness*, Sonja Lyubomirsky says you shouldn't underestimate the importance of small moments of joy. "Positive emotions beget upward spirals. For example, you feel invigorated after aerobic exercise, which boosts your creativity, which gives you a new idea about how to enchant your partner, which strengthens your marriage, which shores up your satisfaction and commitment, which leads you to be more grateful and forgiving, which fuels optimism, which creates a self-fulfilling prophecy, which buffers the sting of a setback at work, and so on. Some of the changes produced by small boosts of positive emotion are small, and some are big, but they add up."

OVERCOMING SELF-DOUBT AS A WRITER

Matthew Kressel

Matthew Kressel is a coder, writer, and has been a finalist for the Nebula Award, the World Fantasy Award, and the Eugie Award. His fiction can be found in Clarkesworld, Lightspeed, Tor.com, Analog, The Year's Best Science Fiction and Fantasy 2018 Edition, and The Best Science Fiction of the Year: Volume Three, and many other places. Matthew created the Moksha submissions system, used by many of the largest speculative-fiction publishers today. He is also the co-host of the Fantastic Fiction at KGB reading series in Manhattan alongside Ellen Datlow. Find him online at matthewkressel.net or @mattkressel.

This essay was originally published on the SFWA blog.

It's become a cliché, the tortured writer beset by periods of debilitating self-doubt. But things become clichés simply because they have been true for so many. Writing, for most people I know, is an experience of few victories and many small defeats. The little victories can make all those defeats worthwhile, but when you're in the writing mode, staring at the screen or paper, slogging away day after day, without feedback, you can often feel like you've wandered deep into the woods without a guide and now you're lost and it's getting dark and there are strange sounds coming from that grove of trees, and at this far out no one can hear you scream.

Eventually, though, you'll find your way back to civilization. You send out that story that you worked on for months, only to get rejection after rejection. You submit your magnum opus to agents and editors expecting high praise only to be met with…crushing silence. The waiting sometimes can be the worst of all.

And it's in these interstitial periods that the most debilitating feelings of self-doubt can occur. We ask ourselves, Am I good enough? Am I smart enough? Did they like what I wrote? Does it suck? Am I a hack? What the hell am I doing all this for? All those things we do to escape our uncomfortable feelings become super tempting: binge television watching, drinking, drugs, sex, anything to escape the Great Uncertainty.

And then your story sells, maybe even to a pro market, and the reviews come in, and everyone loves it, and praises it. And people talk about how it moved them, some cried and read it to their grandmothers, and maybe your story even gets nominated for an award. Maybe you even win that award. And you feel like a million dollars, and you'll never doubt yourself again.

Yeah right.

A few weeks go by, maybe a few months, and the doubts creep back. We say to ourselves, Maybe I was lucky. Maybe the awards system is rigged. Maybe it was only a popularity contest. Maybe that's the best I'll ever do.

It's a vicious cycle, this self-doubt, and it's been my experience that most writers experience these debilitating neuroses in one form or another. A few lucky people I know seem to lack all such self-doubts, but I suspect they're well hidden, that under their confident exterior they too doubt themselves from time to time. Hell, even Stephen King has been known to express doubts about his work.

Whenever I get into an emotional funk, when the self-doubt niggles its way into my psyche, I find that there are some things I do that help brush it away.

Write. Yep, it seems ridiculous that the cure for self-doubt about your writing is to write more, but I've always doubted myself less after a morning where I've written 1,000 words than on mornings where I wrote none.

Remind yourself that many people have it a lot worse off than you. By this I mean that there are people in this world who survive by scavenging garbage dumps to get food for themselves and their children. There are people who live under threat of rape, war, terrorism every single day. Just by having the time to write, you are in an incredibly privileged position. This does not mean your feelings aren't real or are worthless. It just means that you might put them in perspective.

Go do something good for someone else. Give some cash to that homeless guy on the corner. Help a friend move apartments. Call up that family member you haven't spoken with in a while just to say hello and really listen to them You'd be surprised how liberating it can be to get out of your own head, even for a little while.

Remind yourself of all the things you have accomplished. Look at the short stories or novels you published and read the positive reviews. If you're just starting out and don't have this resource, remind yourself that all writers go through an early rejection phase. Stephen King said that he used to keep his rejection letters hung on a spike on the wall, and he had once accrued so many that the spike fell. Consider that next time you get a rejection.

Even veteran pro writers get rejections. I have the privilege to know several top editors in SF and I know for a fact that big names do occasionally receive rejections too. Yeah, maybe fewer than they did when they were starting out; they have honed their skills after all, but they still do get the splat from time to time.

Sublimate your doubt. Use it as a tool. Actors are taught to channel their stage fright into energy, to bring more life to their characters. Writers can do this too. All emotions, all experiences, are food for us writers. Explore that neurosis, go deep into it, and you just might find a well of ideas ready to spring forth. Any human emotion is a treasure chest waiting to be opened.

Talk to other writers. Writing can be an isolating experience. Just sharing your feelings with another human being who is going through the exact same thing can be a cathartic experience for all involved.

Reframe the metaphor. You're writing a story, but what story are you telling yourself about your own life? That you're not good enough? That you're a failure? What if you reframe the narrative into something positive: This is just one step on my journey. All writers go through this. This is a learning experience. The author Tom Crosshill, a good friend of mine, has a TED talk on just this idea. I highly recommend it.

Feed your inspiration engine. Ray Bradbury suggested that writers read poetry every day to whet their writing skills. For me, I find walks in the deep woods inspiring. Or listening to Bach or other music, or reading passages from my favorite books. Pour life into your soul, and you might find that life pours out of your fingers onto the page in equal abundance.

Meditate. By taking aside a few minutes every day to breathe deeply, to calm those racing thoughts, to recenter and refocus, you may find that what seemed so burdensome before is now more manageable. I can attest to ridding myself of many small and large anxieties by simply meditating for twenty minutes each morning. I'm usually sharper, more relaxed, and more clear-headed afterward, a great mind space to be in before writing.

These are some of the methods I use to overcome my occasional feelings of self-doubt. While they may not be ideal for all, I hope that some will find them beneficial.

WAITING, WAITING, WAITING

If refreshing my email, in vain, were a sport I would be an Olympian.
  - Roxane Gay

Writing involves a lot of waiting. It can be especially nerve wracking when you're waiting to hear back on a submission or a workshop application. I'm old enough to remember having to print out a story and go to the post office to buy international reply coupons. It would take slightly longer than forever for the reply to come back from another country. These days things are generally much quicker with the Internet, but you can still wait months or years to hear back from some publishers.

How do you make waiting less anxious? For me, the best way is to start working on my next project. I concentrate on my new story and try to forget about my submission. That's easy to say and harder to do, but if you're excited about your next project, hopefully you'll feel less anxious about the one on submission. If you have lots of stories on submission, it's easier to be less anxious about any one of them.

In *The Charisma Myth*, Olivia Fox Cabane talks about a technique to relieve uncertainty. "Sit comfortably or lie down, relax and close your eyes. Take two or three deep breaths. As you inhale, imagine drawing clean air toward the top of your head. As you exhale, let that air whoosh through you, washing away all worries and concerns. Pick an entity—God, Fate, the Universe, whatever may best suit your beliefs—that you could imagine as benevolent. Imagine lifting the weight of everything you're concerned about—this meeting, this interaction, this day—off your shoulders and placing it on the shoulders of whichever entity you've chosen. They're in charge now. Visually lift everything off your shoulders and feel the difference as you are now no longer responsible for the outcome of any of these things. Everything is taken care of. You can sit back, relax, and enjoy whatever good you can find along the way... The responsibility transfer does not actually dispel uncertainty (the outcome remains uncertain). Instead, it makes the uncertainty less uncomfortable. By presenting your mind with the possibility that responsibility has been transferred, you're putting to good use the placebo effect—the brain's inability to distinguish between imagination and reality."

Most short story markets will give you a rough indication of how long to expect to wait for a response. This is often the editor's best case scenario rather than a realistic estimate. Online submission logging tools like *The Submission Grinder* show how long markets typically take to respond. These times can vary depending on the editor's other commitments and if there are slush readers reading at different speeds. If you get a hold notice, it means more waiting.

Some short story markets will send you a link that lets you check your position in the queue. You should think about whether constantly checking this number makes you happier or not. It can be exciting to watch your story's progress, especially if you're comparing notes with other friends in the queue. But maybe this increases your anxiety. Sometimes it's better to ignore your queue position and only check if you haven't heard back in the expected time. There have been a few occasions where a decision has been made about my story (sometimes an acceptance!) but the email notification has gone astray, so I was glad I checked on its queue position after the expected response time.

Agents also vary widely in how long they take to respond to submissions. Many agents have a *If you don't hear back in x weeks, consider it a rejection* policy. At least with agents, you can send out other queries while you're waiting to hear back.

If your agent is sending your book out on submission, the time you can wait to hear back again varies widely. Sometimes the editor reading it will be widely enthusiastic and respond straight away, but then a final decision takes months (or longer!) while sales and marketing consider it.

Even after your book is accepted, it might be two years or longer until it's released. Traditional publishing often moves slowly. Big publishers want a long lead time so they can slot the book in their advance catalog. Sometimes a small press magazine accepts your story and then it will be a couple of years till the issue containing your story comes out.

If you embark on the self-publishing path, many of these obstacles will be removed. But there will still be things you have to wait for—your cover artist takes longer than you expected, your copy editor has too many other projects on at the moment, the person you asked for a blurb quote is taking forever to get back to you.

The Internet has made many things so much faster that the pain of waiting for responses can feel heightened in comparison. Being able to make peace with the inevitable delays will make your journey through *Submissionland* an easier one.

GRIEF AND HOPE

Photo by Geert Weggen

THE NECESSITY OF HOPE

A. Merc Rustad

A. Merc Rustad is a queer non-binary writer who lives in Minnesota and is a Nebula Awards finalist. Their stories have appeared in Lightspeed, Fireside, Apex, Uncanny, Nightmare, and several Year's Best anthologies. You can find Merc on Twitter @Merc_Rustad or their website: http://amercrustad.com. Their debut short story collection, SO YOU WANT TO BE A ROBOT, was published by Lethe Press (2017).

This essay was originally published on A. Merc Rustad's blog.

Way back when, as a young!Merc, I attended a gun safety class. One session had a slide show about wilderness survival.

A [generalized "average"] human can survive:

3 weeks without food.
3 days without water.
3 minutes without air.
3 seconds without hope.

The point was that if you get lost in the wilderness, don't panic. But it was that last line that stuck with me.

Three. Seconds.

Three seconds without hope.

No one needs a recap on how horrible the political climate is right now. It's bad. It's terrifying.

So many of my friends are struggling and scared and hurting. So am I.

We have already lost people. We will lose more. It hurts

so fucking much to say that. To realize that some of us, when hope is lost, will not be here tomorrow.

Here's a thing about depression. It's inside your head. It's right there, often inescapable (how can you get away from your own brain?) chewing up your thoughts and telling you horrible lies. Depression eats hope. And when the hope is gone, sometimes the depression wins.

I don't know if the three-second example is accurate–it may be a very personal timeframe, or it may not. But the basis is true: we need hope to live.

All of us.

We're storytelling creatures who thrive on narrative. We understand story on an instinctive level. We see and experience and feel, and we weave these things into a narrative: our story, the stories of others, the stories we choose to tell and see and believe.

So let's say that you read a lot, or watch visual media, or otherwise consume a classical idea of narrative structure on one form of sensory input or another. You read and read and read, absorbing all these ideas about how life works, how people work, how emotions work. And sometimes these stories aren't satisfying, or sometimes they are upsetting, and sometimes they are both and you don't know why.

It takes a while to level up enough to be able to decrypt why some stories bother you more than others. And when you get it, you can't stop thinking about it (just like that slide in the presentation years ago).

The stories without hope leave you cold. Or worse, they hurt.

Because here's the thing: we learn from stories. The ones that offer hope? However dark or grim they may be, however much pain and loss they may hold, if they have that hope at the end, these stories tell you: you can survive this.

The ones that don't tell you something equally power-ful: why bother?

(That is a lie the depression tells you, sometimes. "What is the point? Why do you keep fighting? Don't you know you're worthless?" The thing is, depression is a lying liar who lies, but it's very hard to see that, sometimes, or reject the lies.)

"Hopeless" is used as an insult. When you think about it, it's a terrible, terrible word. One who is without hope is one who is unlikely to live.

And I want you–I want all of us–to live.

I found a cache of young!Merc writings earlier this month as I was moving. I glanced through some of them. Laughed at the terrible prose, but a little sadly–because young!Merc was so desperate to figure out how to survive, even if young!Merc didn't know it at the time, and that pain and desperation came out in grim, violent narratives. And yet, in all the darkness, there was always a tiny speck of hopefulness.

Because even young!Merc recognized that they needed that to survive.

If not all stories would give them hope, then they would carve it out of despair and cling to it for all they were worth.

Not everyone needs the same things from stories. Not everyone needs to hear the same thing. Personal taste is personal. That's okay! And 'dark' or 'grim' does not mean lack of hope in a story. It's not a binary. Hope-stories are not all fluff and light.

How do you define it? I don't know. Sometimes that's equally personal.

For me, I can tell you that when everything is dark-ness/despair/grimdark/unhappiness, when there is rampant nihilism and disregard for any sense of joy, that is likely to be a story without hope. And I don't want to experience that.

Look at real life. We have enough fucking horribleness to go around ten zillion times, that I don't want to fight through a narrative that mimics that level of awful and find that none of the struggle mattered.

I need the stories that bolster hope; hope is fighting against the depression and the darkness. It's fighting with everything we've got, in whatever means we can—not everyone can resist in the same way, and that is more than okay. It is necessary. We need multiple paths of resistance; activism is multi-varied, like the people who activate it.

Whether you write, or speak, march or stay back to keep others afloat (and yourself), call on the phone or email, stay low-key to protect yourself and others or shine on the front lines…all of this matters. No one thing is inherently "better" than another. The thing that is most important to know is: YOU matter. You are necessary and needed and I want you to stay, if you can.

Fighting against the darkness and oppression is not always a visible or violent show. Sometimes it is quieter, and just as fierce. Perhaps it is writing fiction that can reach out to others and tell them: you are not alone, and we can do this.

I write; that is part of my resistance against the awful and the dark and despair. I will keep writing.

Ada Hoffmann wrote a brilliant, moving essay "On hope and voices" that I encourage you to read in full.

And art. Art. Please, if you are reading this, keep believing in your art, in your stories or paintings or songs or whatever it is that you do.

We can build each other up with our art, with our will, with our hope, with our fierce and undying courage to resist the apathy and despair.

Hope wants more than three seconds. It wants a lifetime.

Not all my stories are joy and light and happiness. Some of them are dark. Sometimes we need the dark to contrast the things that are brighter.

But when I write, when I consider new stories I want to tell, need to tell, I ask myself, "Can this story help extend those three seconds just a little longer, so the reader can get to the next thing and continue on?"

And I try, I try so hard, to make the answer "Yes."

THE SPACE YOU MAKE FOR YOUR ART

Kate Elliott

Kate Elliott writes science fiction & fantasy. Her series include epic fantasy Crown of Stars and Spirit Gate (Crossroads), the sf series Jaran, YA trilogy Court of Fives, and the Afro-Celtic post-Roman alt-history fantasy (with lawyer dinosaurs!) Cold Magic (the Spirit-walker trilogy). Gender-bent Alexander the Great in space coming soon. She lives in Hawaii, where she paddles outrigger canoes and spoils her schnauzer, Fingolfin, High King of the Schnoldor.

An earlier version of this essay was originally published on Twitter.

It's strikingly clear that many people giving writing advice have never been responsible for the caretaking and emotional support of others and therefore don't understand or take into account what that means in terms of curating energy and time.

So here is some of my writing advice:

Be kind to yourself. Sometimes you won't get the work done you want to do because of circumstances outside your control or just because you are so tired. It's okay. Really, it's okay. Don't beat up on yourself. You're doing your best.

Talent exists, sure, but often it is a word used to create judgments about intrinsic worth. Don't listen to those voices that want to judge intrinsic worth.

Practice, skill, craft: these are all words that frame the act of writing in a more productive way.

Especially if you are in a situation where you are being told by others that it is selfish for you to write or to invest energy in your creative output (when instead you could be caring for or curating emotional labor for others), BE FUCKING SELFISH, my peeps.

I'll take sheer bloody-minded stubbornness and dogged persistence over externally granted labels of talent any day.

Hang in there. No one knows what the outcome will be of any project. And I guarantee that every voice is unique (even if differentially respected). The art you create can't be made in quite that way by someone else.

The process that works for Writer A may or may not work for Writer B. The process that worked for you on Project S may not work on Project Y. There is no correct process. There's what works for you, at this moment, on this day, for this project.

The best way (and in fact the only way I know) to improve as a writer is to do the work. And then do more work. And then more again.

You will walk this path not knowing what lies ahead. No one knows. Go for it.

And in reality, the very skills and practice of caretaking and emotional labor, which so often are dismissed by many as value-less or mundane, as nothing worth considering, ALSO help you as a writer and artist. Take them in, use them. See them as the strengths they are.

So many people are so tired and feel so unseen. The day-to-day struggles are real. Life would grind to a halt without this endless and often unappreciated caretaking work. The space you make for your art (however large or small) matters as part of this work.

THE BALL IN THE BOX

Lauren Herschel

Lauren Herschel is a Canadian marketing and communications professional living in Calgary, Alberta. Originally from Ontario, she spends her spare time volunteering, or hanging out with her two rescue dogs. Lauren has always had a passion for storytelling and people, often sharing ideas and thoughts from her own experiences – from family to pets to grief and kidney donation (and everything in between).

This essay was originally published on Twitter.

I had a moment today when I saw a lady who reminded me of my ninety-two-year old grandma, who even in the early stages of dementia, completely understood that my mom died. I thought I'd share the Ball in the Box analogy my doctor told me. So grief is like this: There's a box with a ball in it. And a pain button. And no, I am not known for my art skills.

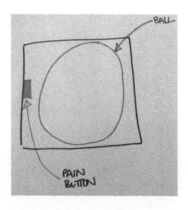

In the beginning, the ball is huge. You can't move the box without the ball hitting the pain button. It rattles around on its own in there and hits the button over and over. You can't control it—it just keeps hurting. Sometimes it seems unrelenting.

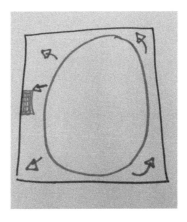

Over time, the ball gets smaller. It hits the button less and less but when it does, it hurts just as much. It's better because you can function day to day more easily. But the downside is that the ball randomly hits that button when you least expect it.

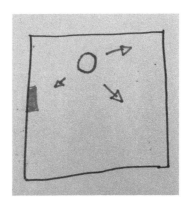

For most people, the ball never really goes away. It might hit less and less and you have more time to recover between hits, unlike when the ball was still giant. I thought this was the best description of grief I've heard in a long time.

I told my stepdad about the ball in the box (with even worse pictures). He now uses it to talk about how he's feeling. "The Ball was really big today. It wouldn't lay off the button. I hope it gets smaller soon."

Slowly it is.

REVENGE IS A HUNDRED DRESSES

Meg Elison

Meg Elison is a San Francisco Bay Area author. Her debut novel, The Book of the Unnamed Midwife won the 2014 Philip K. Dick Award, and was a Tiptree mention that same year. It was reissued in 2016 and was on the Best of the Year lists from Amazon, Publisher's Weekly, Kirkus, and PBS. Her second novel was also a finalist for the Philip K. Dick Award. She has published short fiction and essays with Slate, Lightspeed, Catapult, Electric Literature, Fantasy & Science Fiction, Shimmer, and McSweeney's. Elison is the spring 2019 Clayton B. Ofstad endowed distinguished writer-in-residence at Truman State University, and a co-producers the monthly reading series, Cliterary Salon.

This essay was originally published on Meg Elison's blog.

When I was in the second grade, we'd get a book read aloud to us every Friday, unless we were bad. We were bad all the time, but Mrs. Ellis didn't really want to deprive us. She'd give a little tongue lashing to remind us that we didn't deserve it, but she'd always read the book.

I realized pretty early on that the books she chose always had a tie-in to something that was happening in our school life. We got books about Black history around MLK day, and books about the founding fathers around President's Day. And so it went.

So when she read Eleanor Estes' timeless classic about clothes and bullying, *The Hundred Dresses*, I sat and burned like a tiny flame the entire time.

She was reading it to them because of me.

The Hundred Dresses is a beautiful and sad book for children about a kid who is the very poor child of Polish immigrants to the United States. She has only one dress: a faded, shabby blue number. She wears it every day. When the beribboned rich girls ask her why she does that, she puts on the brave face that most bullied children learn to adopt. She tells them it's a choice. She has a hundred dresses at home, but they're just for parties.

She says, "All silk. All colors. Velvet, too. A hundred dresses. All lined up in my closet."

I knew with the deepening horror that happens at the top of a long fall down the stairs that this book was going to make my life worse. The story ends with the girl leaving the school, because the bullies made life so hard for her. The mean girls feel shame when they see her aspirational drawings of the dresses she dreamed about, because they were so mean to her. They decide they will never be that way again.

My bullies had no shame. They didn't connect fiction to reality, or develop any empathy for me out of their exposure to that Newberry Award-winning classic. I wasn't an immigrant and my father was never going to touch their hearts with his careful dignity in a short letter. I was just a poor, ugly, gap-toothed and freckled kid whom nobody loved. I was shaped wrong and I smelled wrong and moved wrong and always, always dressed wrong. I didn't know how to comb my hair and I never had clothes someone else hadn't worn first. Of course school was hell.

School was hell on a regular day, when the soles of my drugstore sneakers flopped loose from their tops, exposing my sockless feet to rain and cold. But school was a special hell on any day that I tried to do better. If I attracted too much attention by attempting to make a new hairstyle into a turning point, someone would throw gum in my coarse curls. When I wore my Goodwill church dress in an effort to look nice, a group of boys used the white lace front of it to wipe their hands after playing on the tire swing.

I thought about the girl with the hundred dresses all the time as elementary school hell wore on and on. Mostly, I thought about how her revenge was insufficient. I didn't want a well-behaved appeal to pity. I didn't want to draw my dreams into colorful pictures and gift them to my tormentors. I wanted the dresses to be real. I wanted the kind of revenge no one could deny: the kind with a three-foot train. I wanted to show up to school just once in some killer clothes.

I remember notable occasions on my sartorial calendar of misery. In third grade, I got a leather jacket for Christmas from a well-meaning relative. It was white, which I detested. It was not leather, which I learned the hard way. And it had a wide V of fringes from the shoulders out to the sleeves, like I was wearing the entire city of Branson on my back. It was monstrous and I was mocked mercilessly for wearing it.

An older sister sent me a new outfit around the beginning of my freshman year of high school. She had survived a similar upbringing and wanted to try and help make mine a little easier. I remember it exactly: a pair of light-blue straight-legged jeans and a velour t-shirt with stripes in deep jewel tones. I wore it over and over, the way a kid will wear her one good outfit, until it was not good anymore. The crotch gave out in the jeans and the colors faded from the shirt until the velour began to bald. It was nice while it lasted, but the snide comments had just shifted to the sorry fact that I did not have the only acceptable backpack at my school: a Jansport.

It was a reaction to this perpetual disappointment that pushed me toward a goth aesthetic. It was easy to outfit at a thrift store. I would never have the money or the eye for Victorian goth, but punk in black was easy enough. It would excuse my ragged edges and grungy personal hygiene as intentional, and part of an unassailable malaise of the soul.

But *The Hundred Dresses* did not leave me. As I searched the Salvation Army racks for anything benighted, I recall settling my hand on a black velvet sheath dress. It had three-quarter sleeves and a pattern of slim, falling golden leaves. The memory is sharpened by the emotion the dress stirred in me: a combination of desire and fear. I wanted it, but I did not feel I was allowed to want it. I didn't know how to wear it. I would not be permitted to wear it unmolested. I would put it on and everyone would know I was just pretending, that it was only a costume.

I bought the dress.

I put it on at the vanity of a beautiful goth girl, who styled me as avidly as though I were a doll instead of a confused little refugee of style. Terror mounted as she pinned up my hair and painted my face. I would not pass. I did not belong. I wasn't girl enough to wear black velvet to school. I would be weighed in the balance and found wanting. They would see through the illusion to the sexless, shapeless thing within.

It is almost impossible to untangle girlhood from dresses. What is more quintessentially feminine? The dress is inextricably connected to female identity as it is projected and performed in America. I was assigned female at birth, but I always felt as if that had been a clerical error. I was born wrong. Those kids in elementary school had sensed it, and reacted to my weirdness the way pack animals always do. I was not a boy, not a girl. Just a thing that could never dress right and whom no one would ever want to look at. I was deeply, foundationally, unloved and confused. A dress is a small thing. A dress can be everything.

That velvet dress in black and gold shifted the balance

of power within me, and I could feel the tide turning with every step I took. It is a fine thing to land between genders, to be both or neither, or something else entirely. But I had suffered from a desire for girlhood so strong that it was suffocating me. I wasn't girl enough to wear that dress, because I was too much woman already. Girlhood was denied and gone, but I was allowed to be a woman. For the first time, I felt seen in a way I did not think was possible for me. I caught someone looking at my legs and instead of hiding, I knew in an instant that I wanted to pop up my heel and give them something to really look at. My sexuality was mine, because I finally knew what language it spoke.

My body speaks DRESS.

That was the gateway dress. I'll never forget it.

I had thought of dresses as something that happened to me on picture day and holidays. They were always drag and made it more obvious than ever that I did not know how to belong in my body. I didn't know how to wield a dress like a weapon yet. I didn't understand their awesome power to unify my image into as sharp and as neat as a pin. A dress is a perfect thing: a single garment into which you can stitch an entire narrative. A shield and a sword. A statement and a silence.

The girl in the book understood, sketching out the fashions of her dreams. A dress is the ultimate revenge.

That black sheath opened a glittering door for me. On the other side was the brightness of white wedding dresses and the bombshell sexiness of full skirts and low necklines in red. Dresses could make me into a ceremonial object or the priestess who cut its throat. Anything was possible, even making people see me the way I wanted to be seen. Bullies could be silenced. I could escape my misery by shapeshifting in different dresses, putting on different armors of identity. Dresses are drag, but so is everything else. I could use them to tell my story, first to myself and then to the world.

I could project a demure yet subversive sexuality: a vintage cotton frock that nipped in my waist and paired coyly with a little cardigan. I could go full vamp in a scarlet dancing dress with princess seams to accentuate the movement of my hips. I could buy black dress after black dress after black dress, becoming widow and CEO and vampire and slayer and artist and slut and mother superior.

I went mad with power. I discovered a company with a huge online catalog of dresses in every style that would make them custom to my measurements and ship them to me. My dresses were made for my body, and I couldn't keep up with the compliments. I bought and bought, using coupons and loyalty codes and every excuse to gather ever more finery.

A silver evening gown with a deep plunge that requires gaff tape in place of lingerie.

An emerald-green 1940s style day dress with an Empire waist and a fit-and-flare silhouette.

A column dress in black, white, and red that made tourists ask to take pictures with me as though I were a costumed cast member at a theme park.

A wine-red bell-sleeved short-skirted day dress to go with knee socks, boots, and a long vest to make sure people know how groovy I can be.

A purple cowl-neck number that I could picture wearing to court in order to seem trustworthy and truthful.

An asymmetrical dupioni formal with a pattern of huge roses to wear to weddings and dance like there's no such thing as a hangover or sore ankles.

My custom-made red satin wedding gown, trimmed with roses and worn with perfect confidence and knowledge of who I am.

One day I realized I could no longer fit all my dresses

into my closet. It was time to make hard decisions. I hung them up all over the room, trying to decide what was essential and what I could donate or give to similarly-sized friends.

As I looked around the room, I realized I had done it. I had bought enough real dresses to decorate my room with them the way the little Polish girl in the book had been able to achieve only with her drawings.

I was the living revenge of the girl in *The Hundred Dresses*. Silks in every color. Velvet, too. All lined up in my closet.

I can look back over my shoulder and see the rag-wearing kid I used to be, to the girl in *The Hundred Dresses* and the girl who had to endure its reading. I can reach across the closets of time and show them where we ended up. Who we became. What we get to wear. Bullies never go silent, but they do become irrelevant. I can remember every dress I've ever worn, but I can't recall a single one of those kids' names.

Dressing well is the best revenge.

Photo by Devin Cooper

REDECORATING THE PIT OF DESPAIR

I used to be embarrassed because I was just a comic-book writer while other people were building bridges or going on to medical careers. And then I began to realize: entertainment is one of the most important things in people's lives... I feel that if you're able to entertain people, you're doing a good thing.
    - Stan Lee

It seems to me, that if we love, we grieve. That's the deal. That's the pact. Grief and love are forever intertwined. Grief is the terrible reminder of the depths of our love and, like love, grief is non-negotiable. There is a vastness to grief that overwhelms our minuscule selves. We are tiny, trembling clusters of atoms subsumed within grief's awesome presence. It occupies the core of our being and extends through our fingers to the limits of the universe.
    - Nick Cave

Your doubt may become a good quality if you train it. It must become knowing, it must become critical. Ask it, whenever it wants to spoil something for you, why something is ugly, demand proofs from it, test it, and you will find it perplexed and embarrassed perhaps, or perhaps rebellious. But don't give in, insist on arguments and act this way, watchful and consistent, every single time, and the day will arrive when from a destroyer it will become one of your best workers —perhaps the cleverest of all that are building at your life.
    - Rainer Maria Rilke

In *Making Hope Happen* psychologist Shane J. Lopez writes about a patient struggling to find something to say when people asked him how he was. The patient eventually decided upon the answer, "I am working on it."

For most people writing a novel requires a substantial investment of time and mental energy. What happens when you write half a dozen books and no one wants to publish any of them? You spent all that money attending that fancy writing workshop and all your peers have surpassed you. They have agents and book deals and awards and people rave about their writing on Twitter. You've been working hard, you haven't given up, but nothing's happening. Ten years have gone by and friends have stopped asking when your book's going to come out. Maybe you're selling a few short stories, but they get published without much notice. You're never on award shortlists and no one invites you to be in any of the glitterati anthologies. You're going to scream if one more person tells you they found your characters distant. Submitting stories increases your anxiety and getting so many rejections fuels your depression. How do you keep going? Is it really worth it?

One view of the universe is that nothing matters. If you take a long term view, then even the most famous authors will eventually be forgotten. No one leaves a lasting legacy. How much longer will Shakespeare be remembered? 100 years, sure. 1000 years, maybe. 100,000 years probably not. 10 million years, nope. If even Shakespeare is destined to be forgotten, what's the point of bothering? If nothing matters, then logically it follows that it doesn't matter that nothing matters. You won't be around to know that you've been forgotten, so why worry?

The other extreme is reveling in the wonder that you're made from stardust and being filled with overwhelming joy at the sheer improbable miracle of your birth. You know in your glitter-filled heart that each moment is precious and you spend your days visualizing unicorns dancing on rainbows.

Most people aim for a world view somewhere in between. I like to think of myself as combining the boundless optimism of the world's happiest puppy with the world-weary cynicism of a 1000-year-old robot who has seen humanity at its worst. I'm fortunate that I can see the funny side of most situations. I've had friends who lost a parent or a partner and felt even more isolated because their other friends gradually stopped talking to them because they didn't know what to say. Assuming you're not doing it in an insensitive way, being able to make someone who is grieving laugh can be a wonderful gift.

If it feels like you're trapped acting out a role in a student performance of a badly written nihilist play, how do you shift your life closer to The Rainbow Bridge of Sparkly Happiness? If you've ever had to endure a corporate teambuilding exercise, you know that being asked to think happy thoughts can produce undying feelings of hatred in even the most optimistic person.

Most people are familiar with the obvious suggestions. Talk to a counselor. See a doctor. Get more sleep. Exercise more. Eat healthier. Maintain close friendships. Spend time in nature. Value your relationships over material goods. Don't compare yourself to others.

Telling people to think more positively can serve as an excuse for ignoring social problems such as inadequate access to healthcare, discrimination, and poor working conditions. Being able to pursue your dreams is a privileged position. Instructing people to be grateful for what they have can be a tool for keeping oppressed people in their place. If you tell someone they're responsible for their own happiness, this can be empowering and give people hope. It can also make them feel worse. They're the ones to blame for their own unhappiness.

Unhappiness and depression are often linked to societal level problems. The more unequal a society, the more unhappy people will be. One of the best ways to make yourself happier is to improve things for other people. In *Lost Connections*, Johann Hari writes about a study comparing people in different countries making the deliberate effort to make themselves happier. "If you decide to pursue happiness in the United States or Britain, you pursue it for yourself—because you think that's how it works. You do what I did most of the time: you get stuff for yourself, you rack up achievement for yourself, you build up your own ego. But if you consciously pursue happiness in Russia or Japan or China, you do something quite different. You try to make things better for your group—for the people around you."

Writing can be a lonely and isolating profession. Making friends with other writers is one of the best things you can do. Not just in terms of increasing your opportunities, but giving you people to commiserate with. People who understand how hard rejection can be and how sometimes the words just won't come. As terrible as social media can be, it also offers wonderful opportunities to connect with writers around the world.

Johann Hari writes about his discussion with neuroscience researcher John Cacioppo. "To end loneliness, you need other people, plus something else. You also need, he explained to me, to feel you are sharing something with the other person, or the group, that is meaningful to both of you. You have to be in it together—and *it* can be anything that you both think has meaning and value... Loneliness isn't the physical absence of other people, he said—it's the sense that you're not sharing anything that matters with anyone else. If you have lots of people around you—perhaps even a husband or wife, or a family, or a busy workplace—but you don't share anything that matters with them, then you'll still be lonely. To end loneliness, you need to have a sense of 'mutual aid and protection.'"

Having a writing accountability buddy can help. Look for opportunities to apply for a writing mentor. Try starting or joining a local writing group. Yes, there can be problems and they won't always work out, but a good writing community is one of the most valuable resources you can have.

Another way is to reduce your exposure to things that make you unhappy. Take a break from social media. Don't watch TV commercials. Advertising is designed to make you feel your current state is inadequate. Install an Internet adblocker (while being mindful to find ways to support content creators).

Sometimes unhappiness in other parts of your life makes it difficult for you to write. Sometimes it's writing itself and your perceived lack of success making you miserable. Once you send your story out on submission, you have no control on how it will be received. Feeling like your actions are meaningless and you have no control over your destiny is one of the major causes of depression. There's an oft-mentioned study conducted by Ellen Langer and Judith Rodin in the 1970s where nursing home residents on one floor were given greater control of their environment. They were given simple choices such as being able to decide where to put a plant in their room. Eighteen months after the study, the residents who were given more choice had a lower mortality rate than the control group.

Writer Dennis Potter talked about the idea of a *karaoke life*, one in which it feels as though you're singing a song written by someone else. In *Bullshit Jobs*, David Graeber talks about how babies derive happiness from a sense of control and being able to cause things to happen. Psychologist Karl Groos dubbed this "the pleasure at being the cause." Part of what I enjoy about being a computer programmer is being able to create things from writing words and numbers. Graeber's idea of *bullshit jobs* is where someone doesn't have to work hard, is paid well, but is miserable because they know their job is ultimately pointless. This is the "trauma of failed influence", where we know our actions have no meaning. "It begins to give us a sense of why being trapped in a job where one is treated as if one were usefully employed, and has to play along with the pretense that one is usefully employed, but at the same time, is keenly aware one is not usefully employed, would have devastating effects. It's not just an assault on the person's sense of self-importance but also a direct attack on the very foundations of the sense that one even is a self."

Johann Hari mentions a British study which highlighted the importance of being able to make your own decisions. "If you worked in the civil service and you had a higher degree of control over your work, you were a lot less likely to become depressed or develop severe emotional distress than people working at the same pay level, with the same status, in the same office, as people with a lower degree of control over their work... Disempowerment is at the heart of poor health—physical, mental, and emotional... The signal you get from the world, in that situation is, you're irrelevant. Nobody cares what you do."

If lack of control is making you unhappy, try looking for areas where you have more control. If you have the opportunity look for a job that lets you make more decisions, even if they're only small ones. One of the joys of having a garden is being able to see your choices make things grow. If you're tired from lack of control in the responses you get from publishers, self-publishing might be an option. It's a lot of work and isn't for everyone, but having more control over how your book looks and when it comes out, can give you pleasure.

Depression can be so overwhelming that you don't

have the energy or enthusiasm for writing. On Twitter, M. Molly Backes wrote about what she calls *The Impossible Task*. "Depression commercials always talk about sadness but they never mention that sneaky symptom that everyone with depression knows all too well: the Impossible Task. The Impossible Task could be anything: going to the bank, refilling a prescription, making your bed, checking your email, paying a bill. From the outside, its sudden impossibility makes ZERO sense."

Backes recommends to "be gentle with yourself. You're not a screw up; depression is just an asshole. Impossible Tasks are usually so dumb that it's embarrassing to ask for help, but the people who love you should be glad to lend a hand... Take care of yourself, even if that means cutting major corners in your life, or not being 'productive', or living on Netflix and takeout for a while. It's okay. And try to let others take care of you, too, even when you don't believe you deserve it. Remember that people want to help you because they love you, and allowing them to do something for you is its own form of kindness... Whenever you're tempted to beat yourself up for being *lazy*, remember that you fought harder to get out of bed and get yourself dressed today than the average person could even imagine. You're not lazy. Your mountains are just that much steeper. Keep going."

Sometimes making words can just be too difficult. Give yourself the opportunity to rest. You can try again later.

What if you want to be more hopeful about your writing? In *Making Hope Happen*, Shane J. Lopez writes about the core beliefs that hopeful people usually possess. "The future will be better than the present. I have the power to make it so. There are many paths to my goals. None of them is free of obstacles... People who develop these hopeful beliefs are resourceful. They identify multiple strategies for moving toward their goals. They are realistic because they anticipate and plan for difficulties, setbacks, and disappointments. They are resilient because they know that, if one path is closed, another can be cleared."

Lopez also suggests the idea of *nexting*. Focus on the next positive thing. What's the next thing you're looking forward to? What's the next thing you can do to make that happen?

It may seem counterintuitive, but Lopez believes that having an awareness of your own death is also important. "As our time horizons shrink, most people become increasingly selective about the goals they pursue. Dinners with close friends replace late nights at the office. Vacation with the grandchildren takes priority over a business conference... When we perceive that time is short, we invest in people and in our most meaningful goals. Facing death seems to bring us more to life."

Steve Jobs said that "Remembering that I'll be dead soon is the most important tool I've ever encountered to help me make the big choices in life."

Listening to others describe how they felt despair but kept writing can be both good and bad. It can give you a sense of solidarity. You're not alone in your struggles. But it can also make you question your worth even more. *Their circumstances are so much more difficult than mine and they finished a book. Why can't I?* If you can focus on the positives of other people's examples, it can give you a boost of encouragement. Behrouz Boochani is a Kurdish Iranian writer who sought asylum in Australia, but instead has been held in an offshore detention center since 2013. It took him five years, but he wrote a book on his phone, sending it to the outside world one text message at a time. *No Friend But the Mountains* won the Victorian Premier's Literary Award, one of Australia's most prestigious literary prizes.

Stoicism has gained in popularity in the last couple of years, particularly in places like Silicon Valley (resulting in articles being written with headlines such as: *Silicon Valley tech workers are using an ancient philosophy designed for Greek slaves as a life hack.*) There are things to admire about the stoic ideas of focusing on your inner life and not being distracted by material pursuits. The idea of accepting things you can't change sounds good in theory, but it can also be used as an excuse for not trying to change things. In a critique of modern stoicism, Olivia Goldhill writes "there's also something a little, well, eye-rollingly predictable about Silicon Valley elites latching onto a philosophy that teaches them how to accept the things they cannot change. This is a world that's already seen as doing far too little to address real world concerns, is largely populated by privileged white men who are less affected by such issues, and is notorious for being a closed bubble. One Stoic philosopher, Epictetus, was born a slave and wrote extensively on how to accept one's fate."

If all the sparkly happiness and positivity advice is too much, you could read Oliver Burkeman's book, *The Antidote: Happiness for People Who Can't Stand Positive Thinking.* He looks at situations where there's an advantage to thinking negatively. There's a discussion of the 1996 Mt. Everest climbing disaster when eight climbers died. The climbers had pushed on to the summit, despite missing the window in which it was safe to turn back because they believed they could do it. They were caught in a blizzard and died. Sometimes retreat is the smart thing to do.

It's good to be positive and look forward to things. But sometimes hunkering down in the pit of despair can be the safest place to be. Take shelter from the storm, gather your strength, and make yourself comfortable until you're ready once again to flex your writing muscles.

THE OPTIMIST'S GUIDE TO THE END OF THE WORLD

Please don't say 'things have never been this bad' if you actually mean 'things have never been this bad for people like me.'
  - Saladin Ahmed

Hard times are coming, when we'll be wanting the voices of writers who can see alternatives to how we live now, can see through our fear-stricken society and its obsessive technologies to other ways of being, and even imagine real grounds for hope. We'll need writers who can remember freedom—poets, visionaries—realists of a larger reality... Books aren't just commodities; the profit motive is often in conflict with the aims of art. We live in capitalism, its power seems inescapable —but then, so did the divine right of kings. Any human power can be resisted and changed by human beings. Resistance and change often begin in art. Very often in our art, the art of words.
  - Ursula K. Le Guin

I've talked to my father and older relatives about what it was like living in Jim Crow—it seems we're headed back in that direction. And dad was like, 'The way that you stick it to those people is you live your life. You raise your children. You have fun. You sing your songs. You strengthen your culture so that it's resilient against these attacks. And you don't let them destroy your happiness.' This is the lesson I'm still learning as I'm trying to write this book. It's been difficult. But the book is, maybe, helping me learn.
  - N. K. Jemisin

When asked in an interview, 'Are we all doomed?', Helen Garner replied, 'Of course; we've always known it. That's why there's poetry and music, philosophy and religion: so we can bear it.'

I cannot pretend that I am without fear. But my predominant feeling is one of gratitude. I have loved and been loved; I have been given much and I have given something in return; I have read and traveled and thought and written. I have had an intercourse with the world, the special intercourse of writers and readers. Above all, I have been a sentient being, a thinking animal, on this beautiful planet, and that in itself has been an enormous privilege and adventure.

- Oliver Sacks

Many people struggle with how to celebrate joy in their own lives when there's so much suffering in the world. In his book *Utopia for Realists*, Dutch historian Rutger Bregman points out that in many ways the world has rapidly been becoming a better place. "Where 84% of the world's population still lived in extreme poverty in 1820, by 1981 that percentage had dropped to 44%, and now, just a few decades later, it is under 10%... Worldwide, life expectancy grew from sixty-four years in 1990 to seventy in 2012—more than double what it was in 1900... The share of the world population that survives on fewer than 2000 calories a day has dropped from 51% in 1965 to 3% in 2005. More than 2.1 billion people finally got access to clean drinking water between 1990 and 2012. In the same period, the number of children with stunted growth went down by a third, child mortality fell an incredible 41%, and maternal deaths were cut in half... Fifty years ago, one in five children died before reaching their fifth birthday. Today? One in twenty... According to the Peace Research Institute in Oslo, the number of war casualties per year has plummeted 90% since 1946. The incidence of murder, robbery, and other forms of criminality is decreasing, too."

Hans Rosling wrote the book *Factfulness* in an attempt to help correct the outdated world view that so many people have. "Remember that negative stories are more dramatic than neutral or positive ones. Remember how simple it is to construct a story of crisis from a temporary dip pulled out of its context of a long-term improvement. Remember that we live in a connected and transparent world where reporting about suffering is better than it has ever been before. When you hear about something terrible, calm yourself by asking, if there had been an equally large positive improvement, would I have heard about that? Even if there had been hundreds of larger improvements, would I have heard? Would I ever hear about children who don't drown? Can I see a decrease in child drownings, or in deaths from tuberculosis, out my window, or on the news, or in a charity's publicity material?"

Of course many people will point out that circumstances in their own countries have become worse in the last couple of years. It's hard to celebrate the world improving when you and your friends face higher levels of persecution. It seems like one minute marriage equality has been announced and the next there are Nazis openly marching on the streets and reproductive rights are being restricted. How can you remain optimistic when there's so much hatred directed at people you love? And what about global concerns like the climate emergency and mass species extinction?

Australian science writer Tabitha Carvan has an article *How Do We Go On?*, where she asked climate change researchers how they managed to go on in the face of government inaction. Many of the researchers said children and high school students gave them hope. Professor Will Steffen said, "The thing about a complex system, like our societies, is they are hard to predict because they're highly non-linear. It's not simple cause and effect. The state of the system—that is, the neoliberal economic system and our use of fossil fuels—seems so set, so stable, so tough, that nothing's going to affect it. But it's getting eroded from underneath—by the students, by legal battles, by increasing extreme weather events. Where you have a lot of people waking up and saying, *Something isn't right*, that could be the kind of fundamental thing we need to reach the tipping point."

Climate change activist Greta Thunberg says that not knowing all the answers is not an excuse for inaction. "Avoiding climate breakdown will require cathedral thinking... We must lay the foundation while we may not know exactly how to build the ceiling."

Martin Seligman is one of the leading practitioners of the positive psychology movement. His book *Learned Optimism* discusses the research into how people can become more optimistic. "The skills of optimism do not emerge from the pink Sunday-school world of happy events. They do not consist in learning to say positive things to yourself. We have found over the years that positive statements you make to yourself have little if any effect. What is crucial is what you think when you fail, using the power of non-negative thinking. Changing the destructive things you say to yourself when you experience the setbacks that life deals all of us is the central skill of optimism." He talks about the idea of learned helplessness—when you have learned that "whatever you do doesn't matter" and so you give up easily. He compares this to the so-called explanatory style, "the manner in which you habitually explain to yourself why events happen. It is the great modulator of learned helplessness."

Recognizing how you explain events in terms of your responsibility, how long they last, and their pervasiveness is a step towards pushing your thoughts in a more positive direction. Examples of universal pessimistic thoughts are: "I'm repulsive. Books are useless." Making the thoughts more specific results in: "I'm repulsive to him. This book is useless." These thoughts are still negative, but their area of effect has been reduced. *My writing is terrible* becomes *this story is terrible*. Seligman says "People who make universal explanations for their failures give up on everything when a failure strikes in one area. People who make specific explanations may become helpless in that one part of their lives yet march stalwartly on in the others."

For positive events it can help to be less specific. *I'm smart at chemistry* becomes *I'm smart*. Viewing a negative event as temporary makes it easier to maintain hope into the future.

Rather than blaming yourself, in many circumstances it can be helpful to consider the external circumstances. It's important not to avoid responsibility for your actions, but when it comes to things like publishing, there are many factors outside of your control. It's not your fault your story didn't get accepted. There could be many other reasons that don't reflect on the quality of your writing— the editor has different tastes or they've already accepted another story with a similar theme.

If your negative thoughts become overwhelming try distracting yourself when you recognize you're falling into negative thought patterns. Seligman says, "Many people find it works well to wear a rubber band around their wrists and snap it hard to stop their ruminating."

A more effective solution is to learn to dispute your negative thoughts. Challenge your conclusions. Consider the evidence. Are things really as bad as you think? Some self-help advice says to ask yourself what's the worst thing that can happen. I'm not sure of the value of asking writers that question. In my imagination, it's quite possible to see the causal chain between me not finishing the report and the return of the elder gods.

Research shows that keeping a gratitude journal is one of the most effective ways to make yourself happier. Every day write down something you're grateful for. Try not to write the same things over and over ("my kids"), and make your entries as specific as possible. In *Big Potential*, Shawn Achor writes about how this helps your brain "retain a pattern of scanning the world not for the negative, but for the positive first."

Happiness researcher Sonja Lyubomirsky says that for some people writing a gratitude journal every day is too much of a chore. People write the same thing over and over and it loses its value. "The results of my laboratory's gratitude intervention suggested that on average, doing this once a week is most likely to boost happiness, and that's my recommendation to the majority of people. However, on average means that some individuals—and those include you—may benefit most from doing this strategy on an entirely different timetable, perhaps even daily or three times a week or twice a month."

While I was researching this book, I started a gratitude journal. Once a week, I wrote down three things I was grateful for. Now, I've switched to writing one entry every day and I think it's working better for me. Keeping a gratitude journal is one of the easiest steps you can take towards increasing your happiness.

THE SEARCH FOR HAPPINESS EXPLAINED BY A RANDOMIZED HILLCLIMBING ALGORITHM

Happiness is neither virtue nor pleasure nor this thing nor that, but simply growth. We are happy when we are growing.
  - WB Yeats

If you look at life like rolling a dice, then my situation now, as it stands—yeah, it may only be a 3. If I jack that in now, go for something bigger and better, yeah, I could easily roll a six—no problem, I could roll a 6. I could also roll a 1. OK? So, I think sometimes. Just leave the dice alone.
  - Tim from The Office

When I was studying computer science at university we learned about the hill-climbing algorithm. The algorithm looks for the best solution (the highest hill) for a given scenario. The problem is that it can get stuck at a local maximum—there are no higher hills in sight. Maybe there's a higher hill, but it's not visible from the algorithm's current position. To keep looking for higher hills you can introduce a random element, so the algorithm skips around the search space, preventing it from getting stuck at a local maximum. But you don't want the algorithm to be too computationally expensive. When you have a vast problem space, you can't check every position.

Searching for happiness can be like this. Sometimes you find yourself complacent and your life isn't bad, but you wonder what else is out there. Introducing a random element into your life can help you find higher hills. For me, travel has the best way to do this. I think of myself in terms of pre and post my first big solo round-the-world trip.

The hedonic treadmill is the idea that you eventually adapt to changes in your life and return to your normal level of happiness. Buying something you've always wanted might make you happy for a little while, but eventually you get used to it and it no longer makes you as happy. Varying things helps stop you getting used to routine and taking things for granted.

Happiness research is fraught with the problems of subjects self-rating subjective moods and the difficulty in isolating what has caused mood changes. Some research suggests that deliberately seeking out happiness will make you less happy. In *The Geography of Bliss*, Eric Weiner talks about the inherent contradiction between wanting to become happier and the idea that desire brings unhappiness. He mentions a quote from Sundar Sarukkai, "Desire is the root cause of sorrow, but desire is also the root cause of action. How do we counter the paralysis of action when there is no desire to motivate us?" One response is that it's more effective to focus on what brings you joy and do more of that, rather than looking for happiness itself.

Eric Weiner discusses how happiness is treated in different countries. Bhutan is often mentioned in situations like this. The fourth King of Bhutan specified his country was going to focus on raising Gross National Happiness rather than just the economy. In my own travels I've talked to people with different levels of wealth from all over the world. It's easy to fall into the trap of being patronizing when talking about people from less developed countries— *they're poor, but they're happy*. Due to the worldwide impact of movies and advertising, these days many people dream of owning more things. When I arrived in Bhutan, I went to the airport bathroom, and the cleaner was mopping the floor and singing to himself. Then when I met my guide, he and his friend were having an excited discussion about the features of the latest iPhone. A couple of hours later we visited a temple and ran into the King of Bhutan's grandmother who was also visiting the temple. Fortunately I was appropriately dressed for my first encounter with royalty. I was wearing sandals, cheap trousers I had bought in Nepal, and a *Ghostbusters* t-shirt.

Investing time and money in experiences rather than material items will generally make you happier. In his book, *When Likes Aren't Enough,* Tim Bono writes, "the happiness we get from experiences is not bound by the time and space in which they occur. This is why it may be advantageous to have many small experiences instead of only a few large ones. In the New Zealand study that tracked students' happiness levels throughout their vacations, the trip's length had no bearing on happiness. Those who took a quick weekend getaway experienced just as much happiness on average as those who luxuriated for a full two weeks. What matters more than a vacation's length is that we have something to look forward to, and key memories to look back on, with stories to retell and connect with others over."

I'm lucky that I've never had much interest in most designer goods. I've never owned a car. (I've lived in cities with reasonable public transport). Instead, I've spent my money on travel. I usually put a lot of effort into planning my overseas trips in advance. Having something to look forward to makes me happier. One of the first things I do when I get back from a vacation is to start thinking about where I want to go for my next trip. I also make sure to take the time to sort through and edit my travel photos. This helps remind me about my trip and extends my happiness.

In psychology the *peak-end rule* specifies that the most intense part and the ending of an experience play a major role in shaping how we view it in retrospect. Daniel Kahneman and Donald Redelmeier conducted an experiment where they had patients rate the pain they were experiencing during colonoscopy operations. A patient who experienced fifteen minutes of extreme pain is more likely to rate the experience as worse overall than a patient who experienced fifteen minutes of extreme pain followed by ten minutes of moderate pain. The second patient experienced more pain and for longer, but the moderate pain at the end shapes how they remember the experience. In simple terms, *saving the best for last*, is often a wise course of action. I spent two months on a camping trip in southern and eastern Africa. It was wonderful and I enjoy staying in tents, but at the end of the trip, I spent a night in a five-star hotel in Nairobi. I've never appreciated a luxury hotel so much.

Other research says the best way to make yourself happier is to help others. Tim Bono writes, "A nice meal out or a trip to a new place will bring much greater joy in the longer run than acquiring a new computer or a pair of sneakers. But it's not only a matter of what we buy; it also matters on whom we spend our time and money. Investing in others, in fact, is another key way to actively maximize our own personal happiness... People who are striving to improve their own happiness may be tempted to treat themselves to a spa day, a shopping trip, or a sumptuous dessert... [But] they might be more successful if they opt to treat someone else instead. If you really want to be kind to yourself, the best way is by being kind to someone else."

In *The How of Happiness*, Sonja Lyubomirsky recommends seeking out bittersweet experiences. "A bittersweet experience is one that involves mixed emotions, usually happiness and sadness mixed together. Such events are usually characterized by the fact that they will soon end—a vacation, a friendship, a phase of life, a sojourn in a particular place or time. When we are fully mindful of the transience of things—an impending return home from an overseas adventure, a graduation, our child boarding the school bus for the first day of kindergarten, a close colleague changing jobs, a move to a new city—we are more likely to appreciate and savor the remaining time that we do have. Although bittersweet experiences also make us sad, it is this sadness that prompts us, instead of taking it for granted, to come to appreciate the positive aspects of our vacation, colleague, or hometown; it's 'now or never.'"

I lived in Osaka for four years and cherry blossoms are a big part of Japanese culture. There's even a movie named after the speed at which cherry blossoms fall—*Five Centimeters Per Second*. Some of my fondest memories from my time in Japan are going to cherry blossom viewing parties with my friends. Part of the reason the cherry blossoms are so celebrated is that they only last a couple of weeks each year. The transient nature of their beauty reminds people that life is short. Appreciate good things while they last. Making friends while traveling is wonderful, yet also sad, because it's likely I'm not going to have much opportunity to spend time with them in the future.

Reframing things to cast them in a more positive aspect can also be useful. If you sold six short stories in 2018 and then you sold three in 2019, it would be easy to view this as disappointing. Try to reframe it so you focus on the cumulative effect rather than making comparisons. At the end of 2018, you had sold six stories. At the end of 2019, you had sold nine stories. This feels like a simple trick, but it can make a big difference to your happiness.

Reasons to Be Cheerful by Greg Egan is one of my favorite short stories. It's about a man who due to medical complications has software installed which allows him to choose how happy things make him. When he's listening to a song, he can mentally adjust a slider from one to ten which controls how happy the song makes him. When things go wrong and I'm feeling down, I picture a slider in my head and bump it up a couple of points. This encourages me not to think of the event as the *worst thing ever*.

When it comes to happiness and writing, it can be good to try different things. Read and write in different genres. Experiment with different styles, different point of views. Collaborate with other writers. Collaborate with artists. Try writing for video games, for comic books, for role-playing games. Try writing screenplays. Yes, you should focus on what you're good at, but give yourself the chance to experiment.

EMERGENCY BUNNIES

In a recent paper published in PLoS ONE, we demonstrated that people's attention becomes more focused after viewing cute photo images of baby animals. We also found this tendency may facilitate performance of subsequent tasks that require concentration. The result suggests that viewing cute images makes people behave more deliberately and perform tasks with greater time and care.
  - Hiroshi Nittono, Hiroshima University

Positive videos have been found to be one of the strongest good-mood-inducers, however. One review of several studies found that videos had a stronger effect on mood than music or several other mood-induction techniques. This means that videos of things that lift our mood—and cute animal images have been found to do this—can lead to these 'upward positivity spirals' and the life satisfaction and resilience to stress that they bring.
  - Elizabeth Scott

The scientific evidence is indisputable. You should be looking at pictures and videos of cute animals. It can be worthwhile to create an Emergency Bunnies folder on your computer and fill it with images that make you happy. When you're feeling down, venture into bunny land.

There are plenty of Twitter accounts that post cute animal pictures. Try adding them to your Twitter feed. Or create a Twitter list of cute animal accounts you follow. Kumamon is a Japanese mascot (a very friendly bear). Looking at his Twitter account always makes me happy.

SOLIDARITY

SEEING YOURSELF IN STORIES

Likhain

Likhain is a queer Filipina artist and writer. Her visual work is primarily in ink and watercolour and builds on themes of post-colonialism, the apocalypse of surviving empire, beauty and horror, women and monsters, and the defiance of hope. Her work has garnered the British Science Fiction Award for Best Artwork and has been nominated for the Hugo and Ditmar Awards. She lives in Australia with her partner, their Pomeranians, and their princess cat. When not at her job as a designer/developer at a regional startup, she spends a lot of time watching DotA/SC:BW streams and yelling about her faves.

This essay was originally delivered as a guest of honor speech at Continuum.

I'd like to tell you three stories, in the hopes that they speak to you. And this is the first story:

I was sixteen when I learned that I was born to be a villain.

At this point I was a voracious reader of fantasy and science fiction; I'd been scolded several times in class for reading David Eddings instead of taking notes; I'd done the whole "hide novel inside larger textbook" thing. And I was very happy; I had epic stories and interesting characters and amazing worlds to explore. I did not feel any sort of lack.

This began to change on my third—maybe fourth—reread of Tolkien's Lord of the Rings. I was deep in the third book, I think, reading about the histories of Numenor, with Tolkien's sonorous phrasing resonating in my mind; these fair and grave lords of men, tall and gray-eyed; the fair elves, with their flawless faces and graceful ways; and my two favorite characters, both surpassingly fair, Eowyn the White Lady of Rohan and Arwen Undomiel the Evenstar.

That time I paused and was struck with the realization that there was no way I could ever be like any of them—not the Numenoreans or elves, not Eowyn or Arwen. I was not one of those who could have joined the Fellowship, or who could have fought with Rohan or Gondor's armies.

I was on the other side. I was an Easterling. Or I was a Southron, one of the Haradrim. One of the bad guys. The barbarians. One of the nameless, faceless villains in their dark hordes.

It is not only that I was not fair. This went deeper than skin, because it was tied to history, to sociopolitics, to where my country was situated in relation to the rest of the world. To cultural imperialism and language and who got to write stories that would be published and read all over the world. Who got to speak; who got to be heard.

In the books I read, it never was me. I was never one of the heroes. At best I was a sidekick, but most of the time I was an exotic slave or part of the armies of evil. I belonged to the countries that were far away and thus didn't matter; to places that were uncomprehended and therefore savage and hostile, to cultures defined solely by the oppression or brutality of their people.

I did not stop reading fantasy at this point. I read on, even when Daenerys Targaryen emerged to conquer the lands of Essos and that image of her, pale and silver-haired, elevated above a sea of brown bodies, burned itself into my brain. I tried to believe that these things were coincidences, like my white friends assured me. That they meant nothing to me in the real world. I knew this to be a lie, but I swallowed it so I could keep reading the kinds of books I loved.

I'll tell you now what it felt like. It was being a beggar outside a feast, nose pressed against the glass, imagining what it must be like to gorge oneself on all that delicious food. It was hunger that would never go away.

It was acceptance that this was how the white West saw me and people like me. It was a sort of cognizance that this was the way that literature, and indeed the rest of the world, worked. And it was, in the end, a kind of resignation. Yes, I was a beggar, but better to be on the outskirts of the feast than to never know that such food existed at all.

Why am I telling you this? I want you to see where I'm coming from. That for me—and for many others—being part of fandom, loving stories of fantasy and science fiction and horror and all the marvelous genres in between, is not a neutral or bloodless act. That this comes with a price more than time or opportunity or money. That some of us pay this price more often or more painfully than others, not by choice but by necessity.

Stories can cause such harm they make one hate one's skin and people and history; they can justify one's cruelty to oneself and one's fellows because you're all less human, anyway. They can say, with a terrible finality, no. You cannot aspire to respect or dignity, much less heroism. You cannot do great things.

My second story is this: I was twenty-four when I learned that my people understood beauty.

I knew very little about my country's history before the colonizers came. The Philippines was colonized by Spain for three centuries, and during that time the Spanish sought to scour all traces of pre-existing culture from my country. They did a thorough job of it; not much survived, and of what was left most people know very little.

So my history only glanced briefly at what came before the Spanish colonial period. What came before was murky and dark. I have encountered something like that here; the untruth, embedded in so many structures, of terra nullius, where nothing existed before settlers came to birth Australia from this land's unwilling womb. It's a prevalent story, and one that's easy to sell; we started with nothing, we brought civilization here and built this country from the ground up. Look at this arrow of progress.

Because I knew little I grew up with the subconscious belief—and I say subconscious because if you had asked me I would have denied it, for all that it clung to my spine —that my ancestors were primitive savages who knew nothing of literature, or music, or art. That our conquerors had elevated us to a civilized state in exchange for our land, our freedom, and our blood.

Then I went with my partner to an exhibit at Ayala Museum in the Philippines called "Gold of Ancestors". It featured gold pieces from pre-Hispanic times that had been excavated from all over the Philippines, and it blew everything wide open.

Have you ever stood in the middle of a museum floor, hands pressed to your face, trying not to weep aloud? I have. My assumptions of primitive savagery shattered all around me; the depth of my ignorance hit me like a blow. How could I have thought that my ancestors had no imagination or skill? That they had no artistry or the faintest concept of beauty? How could I have bought into the terrible idea that they were savage? How could I have believed that before, there was nothing? In that exhibit I saw jewelry from the 14th century that was so intricately detailed I couldn't imagine how anyone could have done it by hand. And yet my people had.

This was where my art truly began. Until this moment I worked on ink drawings inspired by Japanese kimono textiles and Baroque and Rococo styles, heavily flavored with the fairy tale aesthetic of illustrators like Arthur Rackham. I did my art that way because this is what I admired and knew, while being conscious that it wasn't fully mine. It didn't emerge out of my roots or history; but that was understood because my culture didn't have anything of our own that wasn't externally imposed.

But this—this was something that belonged fully to me and to which I belonged fully. This, too, was a story, because everything in that exhibit was part of a narrative that spoke of artistry where I thought I'd find clumsy handiwork; glorious existence where I'd only known void. This was a story that gave me a foundation I could build upon.

And so I did.

Stories can also heal us. They can close up gaping wounds we don't even know we bear. They can lift us up and say, Yes. Move forward. Through stories we can reclaim histories that have been stolen from us, even if the theft happened centuries ago. And through that reclamation we can begin to confront the trauma of generations of war and colonization and say: yes, we've inherited all this darkness. But we've inherited light, too.

My third story is not actually a single story, but a multitude of stories. And so I can only tell you about a few of them, and you can discover the others on your own.

Because my third telling is one about stories of revolution. In my country's history our revolutions have been fueled by stories; I think all momentous changes are, but especially uprisings against entrenched power. Because how can you persuade people to fight against the current balance of power, if not by telling them a story? That the world doesn't have to be this way; that the world can change.

Towards the end of the Spanish colonial period in the Philippines, two people told two stories. One, the artist Juan Luna, painted Spoliarium, which won the highest honor in the Madrid Exposition of 1884. This story told people that Filipinos—indios, barbarians, who didn't know how to create anything before their colonial masters came to their land—were capable of art that surpassed their colonizers.

The second, the polymath Jose Rizal, wrote two novels: Noli Me Tangere and El Filibusterismo. Rizal was killed for these novels; these stories so inflamed Filipinos and so angered Spanish authorities that their author faced execution by firing squad. When I first read these books I was a grumpy high schooler who didn't see why these books were so incendiary. (Spoiler alert, except it's not really a spoiler because there are no good endings in Philippine colonial history–) They both end badly, with the Filipino heroes either dying, being defeated, or being imprisoned in a tortuous rapehouse. The second book does involve an attempt at a revolution, but it fails horribly.

I grew to understand, though, that succeeding in the fictional revolution wasn't the point. The point was that Rizal held up a mirror to the Philippines of his time, and showed people their true faces. He showed the greed and cruelty of the Spanish friars; he showed the arrogance of the Spanish ruling class; he showed the indifference and incompetence of officials both in the government and in the academe; he showed the injustice of the systems of society, damned if you do and damned if you don't, you'll be crushed under the machine; he showed the thousand slow deaths—by madness, by starvation, by bullets, by imprisonment, by suicide—that countless Filipinos died under Spanish rule. He showed the sheer impossibility of continuing to live in that world.

This is why this story fanned the flames of revolution. This story told people the truth, and the sheer force of this truth drove people to act. If this is the world we live in, I will fight until this world changes.

For isn't that the power of stories, at their core? They change worlds. We're all here because we recognize that. We have all been transformed and shaped and molded by stories. Stories have saved us. They have made us laugh and weep; they have moved us to the depths of our being; they have driven us to make difficult choices and they have fortified us through our darkest times. For many of us, they have affirmed our existence and our right to live. We here are all children of stories.

And we hold on to this—now, more than ever. These are terrible times for so many people all around the world. In my country over seven thousand people have been killed in the past nine months, all in the name of a war on drugs. You don't need me to tell you about how terrible Australia is right now for so many, especially refugees, Indigenous people, and homeless people; or the wars and killings and terrorism attacks all over the world, with countless people forced to flee for their lives, or having to try to fight politicians who are determined to legislate them to their deaths.

And it's hard to think about what we can do in the face of so much darkness and horror. But we can act. For this is the world we live in—fight until it changes.

We can take back the stories. Refute the narrative of hatred and despair. In our actions, in our speech, in our connections with others—we can write our own stories. We can overwrite ethnocentrism and racism with the truer story, that is compassion and a shared humanity. We can shout back at the blaring tale of hateful patriarchy with our defiant resolve to own our agency. We can drown out bigotry and the countless false stories that seek to divide us from each other with our collective story, that stitched together tale-within-a-tale of a community whose members believe that we are not free until we are all free. We can speak up and speak out for the stories stifled by oppressive structures and imbalances of power; we can say these stories have a right to be heard. We can tell, in our daily lives, the story of the person who planted themselves like a tree by the river of truth and told the overwhelming tide of falseness, "No, you move."

And going back to my first story—in our fannish space, as creators and fans, we can change the stories that populate our shared worlds of imagination so that they stop exacting such a toll on people's lives and hearts and do not perpetuate further harm. We can support and nourish stories of reclamation, as with the gold exhibit: to bring people who have been severed from their cultures back to themselves; to center those who have long been shunted off to the margins; to give people who have long been boxed in by toxic narratives the space and freedom to live full lives instead of stereotypes. We can make more space for stories that say: yes! Go and live. Your life matters.

This isn't about political correctness or diversity quotas or agendas. This is about justice. Because we live in an unjust world, where only certain people are allowed to tell stories—are allowed to even have stories. Shouldn't we change that? Shouldn't everyone be given the chance to believe that they, too, can do great things; that they, too, exist, that they matter?

We know how powerful stories can be. We've seen the difference they can make, revealing us to ourselves so that we may act upon those illuminated truths. I ask that we fight, we children of story, to change the stories within us and without us. In our homes and communities and societies and in the quiet spaces of our bodies. We cannot let our stories, these stories of our identities and our histories and our roots, fall silent. Silence is death, and stories support and undergird life.

I'm going to end with a surprise fourth story. This is not mine; it's by Italo Calvino, towards the end of his beautiful book Invisible Cities, where Kublai Khan is speaking out of despair:

> *Already the Great Khan was leafing through his atlas, over the maps of the cities that menace in nightmares and maledictions....*
>
> *He said: "It is all useless, if the last landing place can only be the infernal city, and it is there that, in ever-narrowing circles, the current is drawing us."*
>
> *And Polo said: "The inferno of the living is not something that will be; if there is one, it is what is already here, the inferno where we live every day, that we form by being together. There are two ways to escape suffering it. The first is easy for many: accept the inferno and become such a part of it that you can no longer see it. The second is risky and demands constant vigilance and apprehension: seek and learn to recognize who and what, in the midst of the inferno, are not inferno, then make them endure, give them space."*

That is the core of our work going forward: make them endure, give them space. Hold fast. Uplift our true stories.

Thank you for your time. Maraming salamat po. Mabuhay tayong lahat.

I'M A BIG BLACK MAN WHO WRITES SCIENCE FICTION

Malon Edwards

Malon Edwards was born and raised on the South Side of Chicago, but now lives in the Greater Toronto Area, where he was lured by his beautiful Canadian wife. Many of his short stories are set in an alternate Chicago and feature people of color. Malon serves as Grants Administrator for the Speculative Literature Foundation, which provides a number of grants for writers of speculative literature.

This essay was originally published in People of Colo(u)r Destroy Science Fiction.

I'm a big guy. I'm six feet two inches tall. I'm two hundred thirty pounds. And I'm black.

I'm a big black guy.

That's an uncomfortable image for many people. Mostly white people. But it's a nearly non-existent image when it comes to science fiction writers.

Big black guys are supposed to be athletes.

In 1998, I served as an AmeriCorps VISTA in Billings, Montana, where I worked in an elementary school with at-risk students for a year. My first day, I walked into the cafeteria during lunch time and some kid said (a little too loudly), "Wow, Michael Jordan!"

Makes sense. There weren't too many big black guys in Billings, and the only one he'd ever seen (and remembered) was the greatest basketball player of all time.

Or, big black guys are supposed to be authority figures.

My second year as an AmeriCorps VISTA in Missoula, Montana, I worked at a high school, also with at-risk students. I recruited freshmen to participate in enrichment programs, which meant pulling them out of class. Word got around. One day, an upperclassman asked me if I was a truant officer. Makes sense. The only reason a non-teacher big black guy would pull some of the most troubled (and troublesome) students out of class was to discuss truancy issues.

But big black guys aren't supposed to be science fiction writers.

Makes sense. I didn't know any growing up on the South Side of Chicago. But I knew my sister.

My older sister introduced me to science fiction. I was four-and-a-half years old. She was fifteen.

She was a huge *Star Wars* fan. She'd seen it at the drive-in, where she held a tape recorder to the speaker hanging from the car window so she could listen to her favorite parts at home whenever she wanted. She'd also had so many *Star Wars* toys in her room that going in there was like Christmas morning to four-year-old me.

She had a twelve-inch-tall Darth Vader (cape included). I broke that. She had Luke's land speeder. I broke that. She even had a three-and-three-fourths-inch-tall Lando Calrissian (cape also included). I broke that, too.

I broke everything I could get my hands on.

So she banished me from her room for the next three years. Banishment ended when she went away to college, which meant I could play with all of the toys I didn't break. But there were no toys. She'd taken them all with her.

There were books, though.

I don't remember the first book I grabbed. Probably *Dune*. The Bene Gesserit fascinated me. I—now a little eight-year-old black boy on the South Side of Chicago—wanted to be one of them. When my sister came home from college, I told her. We talked science fiction for days. Even today, we still do.

Back then, my sister wrote short stories and plays, so she encouraged me to write. My first science fiction story was about two astronauts who take a rocket ship to the Moon. One decides to stay, all alone. The other goes back to Earth.

Not all big black guys are athletes. Or authority figures. Or even criminals.

Some of us, like me, are science fiction writers. For many, that's an uncomfortable image.

And yet, we big black guys write on.

Because that is what we do.

THE RACIAL RUBBER STAMP

R.F. Kuang

Rebecca F. Kuang was born in Guangzhou and immigrated to the United States in 2000. She is currently pursuing an MPhil in Chinese Studies at the University of Cambridge on a Marshall Scholarship. Her debut novel The Poppy War *was published by Harper Voyager in 2018 and was a Crawford Award Winner, Goodreads Choice Awards Finalist, and one of* Time's Best Books *of 2018. The sequel* The Dragon Republic *comes out in August.*

An earlier version of this essay was originally published on the SFWA blog.

I've attended two of the better known SFF writing workshops now. Each time I've been one of at most three students of color. This leads to a set of very curious experiences. Being a POC amidst a group of white writers, many of whom started their careers in the wonderful era of Alleged Racial Wokeness, means that I suddenly take on a set of roles that I did not ask for.

It means that I become the go-to consultant for that one student who has decided to play Racial Roulette with each one of her minor characters so that she can tick off her marginalized identity checkboxes.

"I've decided to make the hacker Japanese," she declares.

"Okay."

"Actually, no. Chinese! Should he be Chinese or Japanese?"

"Is the hacker your only Chinese character?"

"Yes."

"And why must he be Asian?"

"Well, I didn't want to make him Russian."

It means that everything I say in workshop gets interpreted through a lens of racial criticism, even though–get this–not everything I say is about race.

"I like that this sorcerer burns someone up," I say in a critique. "That's sexy."

"Yes! As RK pointed out, this sorcerer has magical privilege!"

It means that, for some reason, I am often looked to as the authority on stories about African-American experiences, South Asian experiences, Southeast Asian experiences, and Native American experiences.

"How do you feel about this Hawaiian priestess?"

"Do you think I've exoticized this geisha too much? I just wanted to tell her side of the story."

"Can you help me subvert this Indian doctor stereotype?"

"You're Chinese. Can I ask you about how to write this Korean mother?"

Being the lone POC also means always being the party pooper. It means being considered a weird combination of the Racial Authority Department and the POC who ruins the fun for everyone. Which is a fascinating contradiction, but one that unfortunately makes sense. It shows that many white writers don't take objections about racial representation seriously unless they are convenient.

Because being the lone POC also means keeping silent when everyone in the room wants to watch *Big Trouble in Little China*, because it's "soooo funny!" and "clearly a parody" and "you're not upset about this, right?" (which we can translate as "please don't be upset about this, it'll ruin our fun, why can't you just sit in the corner and be a Good Friendly POC?)

It means that when a racist old white guest lecturer says

my story title sounds like the name of a "laundry company" (think about that for a second) and calls me a "just the cutest little Chinese firecracker," the only support I'll get from my peers are nervous chuckles and slow head shakes. The instructor won't intervene.

It means that the white guy with the MFA gets to write about a Chinese woman who, after being sexually abused by her white "master," commits suicide by drowning herself. The rest of the class admires his artistry. And I am called out for overreacting if I get visibly upset and tell him he has no business telling a story that doesn't have to be told yet again.

What I've seen is that the lone POCs in largely white writing groups often become tokenized faux authorities. We're consulted just enough to give other work a stamp of diversity approval, but brutally marginalized when their opinions become inconvenient.

I imagine this isn't just an issue with workshops. I imagine these dynamics could easily extend to conventions, lectures, and MFA programs. But workshops are the place where many fledgling writers break out their careers, write the first draft of short stories that will make them published, make crucial connections, and get introduced to the SFF community. And workshops are where POC writers learn their place.

At some point, the fatigue becomes overwhelming. It's not fun to be ostracized because you made a white student feel insecure about their work. It's not fun to be the sole spokesperson for your race, much less the spokesperson for other races that you shouldn't be representing. That burden is exhausting and unfair. We weren't hired to teach you.

So, my dear white allies, let me make it a little easier for you.

First, more than anything else, please be willing to do

your own homework. If you want to know about the Asian-American experience, read Lisa Lowe, Sucheng Chan, and Maxine Hong Kingston. Then come talk to me. Prove that you care about my history, and that you genuinely seek to be a better ally. Otherwise, using your POC classmates as an educational tool is deeply disrespectful and often hurtful.

Second, don't roll your eyes every time POC students speak because "it's just another race thing." Don't say that "I don't want to fix that because race really isn't the focus of my story," because you either actively challenge existing hierarchies or you tacitly accept them. Don't mutter that I am just the "social justice warrior" with the nefarious, censoring agenda. Don't accuse me of going on a spiel about racism because I don't know how to critique a work otherwise. Don't reprimand me when I get angrily critical of your work. Trust me. None of us want to be the campus PC police sent to shut down your party of blissful ignorance.

Third, recognize that we can't speak for other POCs. I, for instance, can't answer your questions about the black experience because I am not black. I can't answer your questions about Gal Gadot and whether Ashkenazi Jews are or aren't white. I am not Jewish. I am not black, I am not South Asian, and I am not Polynesian. I don't know. I can read about those issues and try to educate myself, but I cannot speak about them with authority.

Fourth, recognize that you don't get to offload the burden of calling out racism to me. Don't look uncomfortably in my direction when someone has said something cringe-worthy. Don't make me the scapegoat. Say something. Yes, you'll feel awkward. Yes, it might make you unpopular. But you can fly under the radar, or you can be a good ally. Up to you.

And finally, for the love of God, please don't make me

a racial rubber stamp. Writing about race is complex. It takes time, research, and hard work. If you aren't willing to put that in, then please don't ask POC to vet you along on your merry way. Stop asking my permission to take the easy way out. You don't have it.

CULTURAL APPROPRIATION FOR THE WORRIED WRITER: SOME PRACTICAL ADVICE

Jeannette Ng

Jeannette Ng is originally from Hong Kong but now lives in Durham, UK. Her MA in Medieval and Renaissance Studies fed into an interest in medieval and missionary theology, which in turn spawned her love for writing gothic fantasy with a theological twist. She used to sell costumes out of her garage. She runs live roleplay games and sometimes has opinions on the internet. She won the Sydney J Bounds Award (Best Newcomer) in the British Fantasy Awards 2018.

An earlier version of this essay was originally published on Medium.com.

I often get asked by white people how to write about cultures and identities that aren't their own. Here's a rundown of what I recommend for people worried about appropriation and writing outside their identities.

Examine your motives. Why do you want to write about this?

Are you trying to solve racism/sexism/colonialism/heterosexism/cissexism/etc with your work?

As writers we love stories about heroic writers whose work has changed the world. And as such we like to look to our own writing to solve societal problems or raise awareness of issues. And I understand this completely, not the least because I've felt the pull.

But if you're looking to play savior with your words, it's unlikely you will do the marginalized people you are trying to save justice.

And I understand this often comes from a place of good intentions, but there's a reason most of the moralizing plays written by white abolitionists are deeply uncomfortable to read. It's incredibly easy for works looking to play savior to become patronizing or traffic in simplistic stereotypes that ultimately hurt the people they're looking to speak for.

It's not uncommon, for example for a parable about racism being taught via a racist protagonist learning a lesson. But as such, you are still making the reader read about someone being awful to people like them for most of the story. It can reduce those marginalized people to props in the personal growth of your racist protagonist.

It's also worth bearing in mind that many seminal works of anti-racism that white people love, such as *Huckleberry Finn*, are not equally beloved by black readers.

Are you looking to write a story about that identity?

There's a huge difference between writing a story with a diverse cast that reflects the complexities of the world and a story which looks to represent them to the world. The latter seeks to speak for them, seeks to be an exploration about that identity.

It's fine and good to write a story with gay characters if you are straight. I would strongly advise against writing a story that centers on the specific struggles of being gay in an oppressive society if you are straight.

It's excellent and representative of reality to have black characters, but if you're a white writer, I urge you not to try and write the next *The Hate U Give*.

Ask yourself what your story is about.

Everyone worries about getting it wrong.

I often feel people are implicitly asking me for permission. And I understand, there's this weight of expectation and responsibility you want to be free from. I desperately want to write with the freedom I felt when I was ten, when I didn't worry about what other people thought about my work or who was reading it. Self-awareness can be uncomfortable, and you think perhaps this can help you return to that state of grace.

There's no simple fix that can be done once and allow you to stop worrying about cultural appropriation forever. It doesn't work like that.

We all worry about what we write. We all worry about hurting the people we are writing about. Marginalized writers, if anything, worry even more about such because we intimately know the hurt that can be caused, we remember the books that have failed us and the disappointments we have felt. We worry about doing our own cultures and subcultures justice. We worry about accidentally confirming or validating stereotypes and further entrenching them in our culture. If we are diaspora, we worry about our authenticity and being estranged from those cultural impulses.

So you, worried writer, are not alone in this.

We all worry and I sincerely believe this is a good thing. It is what keeps us honest. It is what makes us do better.

Stop looking for rules.

There's a tendency in humans to desire rules, of what should and should not be permitted. It's very easy, however, once you've reduced things to rules, it is all too easy for some to forget why something is bad. Some will begin to argue that the rules seem arbitrary.

It is easy to point out loopholes and exceptions to rules. But it was never about the rules to begin with. And it is the constant societal repetition of certain stereotypes and ideas that creates harm. Symbols gain meanings. A single instance will often seem trivial. The point, however, is not contributing to that deluge and as such you have to understand these things in aggregate, as patterns.

Stop trying to find equivalents. Stop it with the thought experiments about likening cheongsam to lederhosen or asking if blackface is the same as a child wearing a long-sleeved Thor costume that has bare arms with white skin.

These things come back down to the power and privilege of different groups within a society. It's about history and repetition and cultural memory. Symbols and actions and tropes all gain meaning through the people who have used them, who have weaponized them before.

This isn't about you.

Stop worrying about people criticizing you.

I know it feels bad to be shouted at when you have good intentions. I know you want to shield yourself, to point to the people who liked your book, to point to all the due diligence that you have done, that any mistakes that have been made can't possibly your own.

The hurt cultural appropriation causes is real and the best way to avoid it isn't to approach this defensively. This isn't about how to lawyer up before the verbal accusations begin.

Worry about the harm you can cause and understand it. Listen and believe people when they say something is bad.

And yes, there isn't always consensus on if something is bad. Works that are beloved and inspiring to some are hated by others. No culture is monolith. The lack of consensus does not make the hurt any less real.

It's possible for some people to love your work and for others of the same marginalization to hate it. It's not your place to demand those who love your work to defend it. It's not your place to demand consensus.

Only by actually understanding this can you avoid these issues.

And more importantly: never mistake the confidence necessary to write as reason to shut down criticism.

If you're doing research, be aware of who wrote the books and articles you are reading.

Be aware there are many people who are more written about than writing. This isn't to say that only portraits from within a culture are accurate or insightful, but if your only sources are written by outsiders, then it's easy to pick up those unconscious biases. There will be misconceptions that have been rattling around that literature for years because people are citing each other in an echo chamber.

For example, if you're writing about Norse myth, know that Nazis have an intense interest in it and there are many racist and sexist interpretations out there. This isn't to say you shouldn't write about Norse myth but that you should check your sources.

If you're writing about ancient Egypt, make sure you're reading more than just Victorian accounts of adventure archaeology. If you're writing about Irish myth, maybe throw in some writing that isn't by Americans.

And this all applies all the more if you're looking to write about living people and living traditions.

Also, be aware of the purpose behind a book. Things written for tourists, for example, will often be looking to package the culture in a way to appeal to the traveler, to sell them that experience. A culture is more than lists of foods and festivals.

. . .

Marginalized people often have a culture invisible to the dominant one.

One of the reasons why marginalized people are so able to write about the dominant culture is that we often don't have our own fiction, we are used to empathizing with the Aragorns and the Tony Starks.

But more than that, marginalized cultures are often depicted in problematic ways or just not depicted at all.

This isn't for a second to suggest they are fundamentally different or alien in some way, but there will likely be things you're not familiar with. Many white people aren't aware about the discussions around the "double eyelid", for example, and why eye shape is a complex issue to East Asians. People who aren't black probably don't know about the hair chart, or how natural black hair has been deemed unbeautiful and unacceptable by the dominant white society in America.

So when I urge you to research, these are the things you should look for.

Be aware of tropes that have gone before.

If you're writing about a culture that's not your own, it's possible you're not aware of those tropes about it and within it. You won't necessarily know what's been done to death and what you should perhaps avoid.

For example, many white women are sick of being the love interest. But for black women, being seen as desirable is still rare in fiction.

And remember the opposite of a stereotype is likely also cardboard nonsense. So whilst trying to avoid the evil, inhuman savage, be aware that the opposite stereotype of the noble savage is equally insulting and two dimensional. The docile doormat woman is annoying and ubiquitous but so is her opposite. These dichotomies are themselves toxic and should be torn down.

Pay the people who are teaching you.

There are a myriad websites and resources on the internet. *Writing the Other* is an excellent place to start, they have a specific section on cultural appropriation that I recommend you read. Attend a workshop.

Many of these resources are available for free, so consider contributing to their patreons or ko-fis. Buy their books. This is labor and they deserve to be paid.

Raise up marginalized voices.

Returning to the first point about wanting to play savior with your own writing, remember there is more that you can do than just write about something. Don't set yourself up as a spokesperson.

Tell people about marginalized writers' books. Retweet their tweets. Cite them as your sources. Recommend their books to your friends. Include their books on lists you write. Review those books. Promote them.

EL MAYARAH - STRONGER TOGETHER

Mary Swangin

Mary Swangin is the Senior Editor for On Comics Ground and a comic super fan who spends way too much time and money on them. She's blessed to have a beautiful wife who tolerates her many shenanigans and a pet ferret who tolerates her existence. They reside in the Midwestern United States on the prairie lands of Indiana.

This essay was originally published on Twitter.

So, I want to tell you all what happened in the store today. It's probably the single greatest moment I have ever experienced working here.

After the usual Saturday rush, a teenage girl comes in. She looks absolutely terrified and when I greet her she jumps.

She starts going up and down the new release wall and the poor thing looks completely overwhelmed.

So, I make my way over to her and ask if I can help her find anything. She quietly admits that she was looking for *Supergirl*.

We're walking to the Super area when I ask if she watches the show. She smiles a bit and nods. Says Alex is her favorite.

I mention that I'm a huge #Sanvers shipper and the poor thing just breaks down in tears.

I'm trying to figure out what the hell I did to upset her. She's crying and I'm freaking out.

After a minute or so, everything clicks. I'm staring down a crying baby gay. One who was having some big issues.

I tell her that it was hard for me when I wanted to

come out too. She finally stops crying and asks me if it gets easier.

We sit at the coffee bar and talk for a while. She tells me that after seeing it all over Tumblr she binged *Supergirl*.

And when she got to Alex's coming out arc was when things hit her.

She tells me that she wanted to kill herself for so long and that she tried but just made herself sick.

But as Alex's arc continued she started to see that she could be happy, that she could be loved.

She didn't want to die anymore. For the first time, she didn't want to die because she got to see Alex be amazing and be queer.

She said she came to the store hoping to find something to get her through the hiatus, so she wouldn't fall back in depression.

She had no idea gay comic characters were a thing, but wanted to try. I tell her about *Batwoman*, *Midnighter*, and *Renee Montoya*.

I pull out my starters which are *Batwoman: Elegy*, *Midnighter*, and *Gotham Central*.

I also dug up a copy of *The Adventures of Supergirl*, just to get her through.

She had enough cash for one and was torn on which to get. She decides on *Batwoman* and asks if I can hold the rest for a while.

I was having an internal crisis at that time, because this kid was me years ago. I was barely holding off my own tears.

I ended up buying the other three for her and I make her promise me that in ten years she'll help another queer kid.

So, I'm out sixty bucks and I cried in the bathroom for an hour but it was damn worth it.

HOW TO WRITE TRANS, NONBINARY AND/OR INTERSEX BACKGROUND CHARACTERS —AND WHY

Bogi Takács

Bogi Takács is a Hungarian Jewish agender trans person (e/em/eir/emself or they pronouns) currently living in the US with eir family and a congregation of books. Bogi writes, edits, and reviews speculative fiction and poetry. E is a winner of the Lambda Literary award for editing Transcendent 2: The Year's Best Transgender Speculative Fiction, and a finalist for the Hugo and Locus awards. Bogi talks about books at www.bogireadstheworld.com and you can also find em as @bogiperson on Twitter, Patreon, and Instagram.

An earlier version of this essay was originally published on Twitter.

We often don't see transgender, nonbinary and/or intersex characters in stories; even in the background. It is possible to offer casual inclusion even when gender or sex is not a main part of a story—but there are potential pitfalls to avoid. This essay is an expanded version of one of my popular worldbuilding threads on Twitter. It is also based on my experience as an editor of multiple trans and/or gender-focused short story anthologies, and a reviewer of speculative fiction and poetry of various lengths. The patterns I will discuss are general, so I'm not going to single out any particular book or story. Instead, I will use examples I created for the purposes of this essay.

Oppressive universes?

When it comes to worldbuilding, it is important to

distinguish between the *setting* being cissexist, and the *writer* being cissexist. It is possible to write about a cissexist world while not being cissexist – technically, most contemporary fiction set in the real world qualifies as having a cissexist setting. But there is also a fair amount of speculative fiction that would fall under this rubric.

Writers being cissexist on purpose probably do not like to read advice articles! But to avoid being accidentally cissexist, we need to discuss writing cissexist *worlds*. Probably the most common setup for such a setting looks like this:

- Women do X activity
- Men do Y activity
- There is no visible pathway of transition between these categories
- There is no visible way of not being a woman or a man

This is somewhat of an oversimplification; each of these points has many gradations. For example, people might be able to transition, but face large barriers while doing so—again, as we can see in our own world. But in speculative fiction, and especially fantasy, the lines are often rigidly drawn. Let's imagine a setting where men do water magic and wear blue robes, while women do fire magic and wear red robes. With this kind of setup, we really need to consider background characters. If you are showing a crowd, where are the purple robes? The gray ones?

You need to consider where trans and/or nonbinary people fit in; and depending on your precise setup, probably intersex people too. Even if you only answer this question in a sentence or two, or in a small aside, it will benefit your writing and worldbuilding. Otherwise the incoherence might be easily spotted, and has the potential to be casually hurtful to your readers.

I'm not saying "Don't feature gendered aspects in your worldbuilding" at all. You can absolutely have gendered aspects. You can have women's and men's cultural items, events, and so on. But you will want to think about how trans, nonbinary and intersex people fit into this, even if you're not showing it beyond a brief paragraph.

Some questions you can think through: Is it possible to transition between the two binary genders? Is it possible to not fit into the two binary genders and/or sexes? How does that work in practice? What are the associated attitudes, cultural aspects, and so on? Note that this doesn't mean that transition has to be easily accessible or widely available. Your fictional society can be actively oppressive. But it will help you as a writer to consider that oppression, or the lack of it. You can also think about changes, in a process-oriented perspective. Is your world moving in a specific direction? Are barriers being lifted, or conversely, are more barriers springing up?

Often writers do not think about how a binarist and trans-exclusionary society can be actively oppressive. Beautiful men's and women's traditions! Yay! This can be written well, but what happens when someone doesn't fit into the two boxes?

Surface vocabulary versus structural change

One major issue I see increasingly frequently is when this kind of structural exclusion is built into the setting, but combined with trans-inclusive phrasings on the surface. If you say, for example, "men, women and other people," you need to have some idea about the "other people." Who are they? Where are they? Are they hiding out of sight, uncomfortable in their red and blue robes? Forced into wearing red and blue robes?

This is a difficult issue, but it needs to be said, over and over again: editors are increasingly educated about inclusive phrasings *on the sentence level*. But many of them do not think about the implications *on the structural level*. So we see writing published that works well, taken sentence by sentence: writing that doesn't reduce e.g., pregnancy to women, that doesn't reduce people to men and women, and so on. But it breaks down when we get to the structural aspects of worldbuilding. (This is true not only of gender- and sex-related inclusion, but across the board—I frequently see it related to colonialism, which would be an entire separate discussion. These days, the Anglo-American mainstream of speculative fiction tends to eschew the surface vocabulary of colonialism, while keeping colonialist structures essentially intact in worldbuilding.)

If your world has fancy nanotechnological shapeshifting, where are the trans people? Will people experiment with their bodies and their gender presentations casually using this futuristic technology? These kinds of settings tend to tilt in favor of such self-experimentation, and show body modifications in detail, but often we still don't see trans people on the page. Where are they? And why?

Not all trans people transition, and transition can take various forms. But many people will often transition despite huge obstacles; and this has been true historically too. Intersex people, likewise, have existed since time immemorial. You need to think about both groups; and also that intersex people can be trans, too.

Brutalizing your characters

A further important aspect is that if you are a cis writer, you probably don't want to write about a crushing oppression specific to trans people; and if you're not inter-sex, you also don't want to have the same negative focus on intersex people. Writing about brutal marginalization of any kind of minority group is difficult coming from an outsider, and there are immense pitfalls to navigate. So most writers steer away from such stories, and with good reasons. But you don't want to *casually imply* a crushing oppression either! A lot of simplistic gender- and sex-related worldbuilding implies just that. If there are no trans, intersex, nonbinary etc. people visible and known, they (we) are probably in hiding, or actively kept from visibility.

An example from this world: there are a lot of young people suddenly transitioning after becoming of age. This doesn't mean they all of a sudden became trans! It simply means that their parents are no longer able to force them to live as their birth-assigned gender.

We are everywhere

People who do not fit into rigid concepts of gender and sex have never been particularly rare; it is a modern Western assumption that we are. A wide variety of cultures have, and have had different concepts, including both of my own. So you probably do want to show at least some people who are trans, nonbinary, intersex and so on—even if only as background or minor characters. We are desperate to see ourselves in fictional worlds. Even a few sentences demonstrating that we exist in the story universe can make us happy—or at the very least, *relieved*.

A little bit of thoughtful worldbuilding will go a long way, even if this is by no means the focus of your book. Just be mindful that if the characters make present-day "pro-gressive" statements, the social structures need to reflect that (they absolutely can!), otherwise their words will ring hollow. With the above caveats about highly focused and intense oppression, these social structures can be any kind. It is always possible to be more inclusive. Sometimes I see writers concoct elaborate scenarios to explain why trans and/or nonbinary and/or intersex people can absolutely not exist in the setting they are developing. If you feel inclined to do this, stop for a moment and consider why you are writing this story. Gender-and sex-marginalized people have lived both historically and in the present day under oppressive conditions, have often faced both figurative and literal erasure, and yet still remain. Showing persistence and survival, but also just as much thriving and happiness, can help ensure your characters do not remain two-dimensional even if they do not assume a major role in the story.

Good writing and happy worldbuilding!

THE VENICE OF AWKWARD COMPARISONS

Message movies, especially the ones that we don't think are message movies, are the ones where the message is so close to what we're used to the real world telling us that we assume it's like real life. Every piece of art is someone communicating an idea to you.
- Boots Riley

If you do much traveling, you'll soon discover there are 432 Venices of the North, 254 Venices of the East, and 612 Parises of the East. Well, maybe that is a slight exaggeration, but there are *Wikipedia* pages devoted to listing all the so-called Venices of the North and East.

Comparisons are where a lot of people get themselves in trouble. They compare themselves to others and feel bad. Or they make insensitive or racist comparisons.

The temptation to compare is almost irresistible. Metaphor and simile are convenient methods for explaining complex ideas and they're an important part of creativity. Sometimes they can be valuable as explanations, giving a name makes it easier to recognize similar cases. *Spoon theory*. *Missing stairs*.

Comparisons can reduce arguments to lazy stereotypes though. *Men are from Mars. Women are from Venus*. It's a problem if people are only familiar with a single instance so they compare every new example to the obvious case. This can be particularly hurtful when applied to people. Every new black woman science fiction writer is the next Octavia Butler. Chimamanda Ngozi Adichie has a TED talk on *The Danger of a Single Story*.

People can get into trouble when they compare what they're doing to stereotypes of other cultures (even excluding issues of cultural appropriation). *I'm opening a restaurant with Chinese food, except it's clean and healthy.*

People want to show solidarity and compare someone else's problem to something they've experienced. They want to be empathetic and show they understand, but it can come off as clueless, especially when their friend is experiencing something they'll never have to deal with.

Writers can get into trouble because they didn't consider the comparisons people will make. This is especially relevant when it comes to science fiction and fantasy. Maybe you've developed a fictional world and as far as you're concerned it has nothing to do with real world history and readers shouldn't look at it that way. The slaves in your world are happy to be slaves because that's the way they evolved. You don't intend it to be a commentary of the history of slavery in the real world. Maybe your fantasy empire colonizes other nations and you show all the benefits the conquered people get from belonging to an empire. You find yourself thinking that readers shouldn't infer anything about your opinions on the history of colonialism. Maybe your brave explorers encounter savage tribes in the wilderness and manage to outsmart them. You don't think that has anything to do with how you view indigenous people in the real world. Unfortunately, it doesn't work like that. In the same way it can be intuitive to use comparison to explain a concept, readers are going to compare your story to their own experiences. Try to consider how people will compare the events in your fictional world with the history of our world.

It's difficult not to compare yourself unfavorably to others. You're supposed to have role models to emulate, which means comparing how they did things to your own progress. Especially with social media, it's tempting to compare your rejection letters with your friends posting about how tiring it is to sign autographs in a stadium for three days without a break.

Tim Bono says that happiness is linked to being able to derive worth from your own standards rather than comparing yourself to others. "One of the differences between happy and unhappy people seems to be the standards they use to judge their abilities and feelings of self-worth. Happy people are guided by internal values and standards, and are largely unaffected by others who may be outperforming them. For unhappy people the opposite is true. They are highly sensitive to how others are doing and will feel good about themselves so long as they are doing at least a little better relative to those around them. It doesn't matter how high their starting salary is, what matters is that what they have is more than what everyone else has."

Barry Schwartz discusses the problem in *The Paradox of Choice* and writes that because society rewards some people with access to the best universities and jobs, it's hard to avoid comparing yourself to others. He mentions studies where people are asked whether they would prefer to earn $50,000 a year with others in their office earning $25,000, or to earn $100,000 a year but other people are earning $200,000. "In most cases, more than half of the respondents chose the options that gave them the better relative position."

One way to try to minimize your unhappiness at how you are doing compared to others is to keep a gratitude journal. Make the effort to record the good things in your life. Comparing yourself to others is another situation which doesn't have an easy answer, but at least if you're aware of when you're doing it, you can reduce its influence. Try to remember there's only one Venice. Focus on each city's unique qualities.

FRIENDS AND NEMESES

THE GREAT GREEN DEMON

Fonda Lee

Fonda Lee is the author of the Green Bone Saga, beginning with Jade City, which won the World Fantasy Award for Best Novel. She is also the author of the acclaimed young adult science fiction novels Zeroboxer, Exo, and Cross Fire. Fonda's work has been nominated for the Nebula, Andre Norton, and Locus Awards, and been named to Best of Year lists by NPR, Barnes & Noble, Powell's Books, and Syfy Wire. She won the Aurora Award, Canada's national science fiction and fantasy award, twice in the same year for Best Novel and Best Young Adult Novel. Fonda is a recovering corporate strategist, black belt martial artist, and action movie aficionado residing in Portland, Oregon. You can find Fonda online at www.fondalee.com and on Twitter @fondajlee.

This essay originated as a series of Twitter posts.

Let's talk about the great green demon that haunts any creative career: professional jealousy.

If you're a writer (or an artist of any sort), you cannot escape the demon, but you have to be careful not to let it eat you alive. Publishing is not fair. It is not a meritocracy. Talent, hard work, and perseverance are all important, but luck and timing and other random factors also play a huge role. Sometimes they seem like fate, like the unknowable will of the gods.

I spent ten years in corporate America before becoming an author. I can't remember ever being jealous of my office coworkers. Sure, some of them had bigger offices and salaries, but I knew *why*. I knew what I needed to do in my job if I wanted to get to where they were.

Artistic fields are not like that. Success, when it comes,

seems random and opaque. Why is this book so successful, when others like it aren't? Why did that author get a million dollar deal? Worst of all, sometimes you don't even know what *you* need to do to meet your own goals. Because different things work for different people, you'll find yourself questioning everything you do. If only I could write as fast as so-and-so. If only I was as good at social media as so-and-so. If only I could write about "important topics" like so-and-so. And on it goes. Social media makes it exponentially worse. Struggling with your project? Take a break to check Twitter and read about the latest movie option, the latest six-figure book deal, the latest NYT-bestselling debut! It's terrible for morale, and yet we all do it.

And sometimes we're friends with those people! We hang out with them online and in person, we celebrate their successes, we're genuinely happy for them—and privately, we struggle with the green demon. I'm jealous of some of my friends; I'm sure some of them are jealous of me. It's the nature of this field: There will *always* be someone more successful than you. There will *always* be something that feels frustratingly out of your reach. You'll watch other writers land the agent, book deal, award, or sales figures that you'd sell your kidney for. It's okay to admit you wrestle with the green demon. The danger is in letting it eat away at your own sense of worth as a creator, to affect your relationships, to suck the joy out of your art. It's extremely hard to train yourself out of the sense of competitiveness and comparison that we're taught to value through school and sports and non-creative work environments. But it's also extremely important to artistic and mental well-being.

Rather than pretend it doesn't exist, keep the green demon in a cage in the corner. It's okay to let it out briefly once in a while to read *Publishers Weekly*, gripe to your spouse or friends, or admire someone else's signing line.

Then back into the cage it goes, so you can get work done. When the green demon snarls from behind its bars, I try to say, "Yes, so-and-so author or such-and-such book is doing better than mine. Am I doing okay, though? Am I putting in the effort? Am I writing what I'd want to write if I was the only author on earth and no one was looking at me?" Usually, that helps my green demon settle down. Your mileage may vary. But when you struggle, know that you're not alone.

I WANT MY FRIENDS TO SUCCEED, BUT NOT AS MUCH AS I DO

I just want to remind you that what you see is oftentimes a highlight reel. What someone reveals on social media can still be sincere, but it is curated. Nothing is overnight. Nothing is guaranteed.
  - Roshani Chokshi

My nemesis is busy being beautiful and successful. That's ok. I am busy plotting and implementing her downfall. It's a multi-year plan but I am putting in the time. It's fine.
  - Roxane Gay

Famous writers are often asked for their most important advice for beginning writers. The most common responses are to read more, write more, read outside your genre, to believe in yourself, and to not give up. These are all good things, but one of the best things you can do for your writing career is to make more friends. This is not about networking opportunities, it's that other writers can encourage and support you when you encounter setbacks. The downside is that it's easy to become jealous of your friends. You all attend the same writing workshop and your friends get agents and book deals and you haven't even had a story published yet. You want to be happy for your friends, but reading about their success makes you feel bad.

Try to be happy for your friends. If you've ever seen another writer act badly because they were jealous, use them as a negative role model—you don't want to be like them.

Don't try to diminish your friend's success. Even if you feel it isn't fair that they've got a book deal and you haven't, offer your congratulations. Don't say hateful things like suggesting they have it easy because they're from a marginalized community and #OwnVoices stories are trendy right now.

It can help to remind yourself that almost everyone is affected by doubt. Maybe your friend's book is on the bestseller list, but they feel like they've been scorned by reviewers.

What happens if you have friends who try to diminish your success? You get a story accepted and they say that's nice, but they wouldn't bother submitting to a market like that. Or they cheerfully point out bad reviews of your book. The right action depends on the circumstances and how close your friend is. Tell them you don't appreciate their comments. Maybe they haven't even realized how jealous they are. If they keep being deliberately nasty, consider removing them from your life.

If it's all getting too much, take a break from social media. Look through your *Awesomeness Dossier* and contemplate all the amazing things you've achieved. If you've had things published, take a moment to remember that even if you're feeling down about your career, there are unpublished writers who are jealous of you.

Another alternative is to adopt a nemesis. Make a friendly rivalry out of the situation. An article in *The Atlantic* by Taylor Lorenz looked at nemesis Twitter and pointed out that having a rival can spur you on to greater performance. "One 2014 study found that long-distance runners are about five seconds per kilometer faster when one of their top rivals is in the race... Declaring the proper nemesis is key. Ideally you'll find someone just slightly more successful than you are. You don't want to be punching down. And it's best to keep the name of your nemesis private. Running around talking trash about someone on the internet could lead to a very awkward encounter at a party or to getting reprimanded at work. Having multiple nemeses can be useful. You can have a work nemesis, a yoga nemesis, and more... And remember to keep the competition positive."

Roxane Gay regularly tweets about her nemeses. "Having a nemesis is emotional catharsis... I don't really want bad things to befall them beyond say, papercuts and abject failure."

There will be many times when it's useful to ask for help. You need advice. You'd like feedback on a story. You want people to come to your book launch or signing. You need to raise money to attend an international workshop. Some people feel hesitant to ask for help and don't want to impose. Others have no qualms about spamming everyone they've ever met with demands to contribute to their crowdfunding campaign or vote for their book in an online poll.

It's important to ask for help, but how much is too much? This obviously varies by situation and person. When it comes to asking people to buy your book or support your crowdfunding campaign, a good general rule is to let people know you're looking for support, but don't directly pressure individuals to give you money. Most people want you to succeed, but not everyone has money to spare. Even if it's only a few dollars, it can add up if you bought books from everyone you knew online.

If you're uncomfortable with the idea of asking for anything at all, it's worth watching Amanda Palmer's TED talk on *The Art of Asking*. She says that artistic endeavors should be valued and that stories and art are worthy of payment. "Asking makes you vulnerable... Through the very act of asking people, I'd connected with them, and when you connect with them, people want to help you."

What about when you need to ask someone for a personal favor? You think they'd be the perfect person to write a blurb quote for your book. Most people want to help their friends and colleagues, and in many cases they'll be flattered to be asked, but people are limited by time. Most writers can't keep up with all the books they want to read and have their own deadlines, so maybe they can't make the time to read your book. In most cases, it doesn't hurt to ask, but don't be upset if people say no. They don't owe you an explanation. Thank them for their response and move on. Some people don't like saying no, so they simply won't reply. If you have an agent, getting them to ask for blurbs can be one way to avoid the awkwardness of people turning you down.

If your first interaction with someone is asking for a favor, it can leave an unfavorable impression, especially if people think you're only interested in what they can do for you. If someone accepts your friend request, don't immediately send them an invitation to like your author page. Respect how people want to be contacted. If an agent has asked people to send queries to their work email address, don't send them to their personal email.

Don't ask author friends if you can have a free copy of their book. Don't ask someone you've just met to read your manuscript. Don't email people to ask them things you could have easily looked up online. Try to avoid asking questions that are too general (*Please tell me the secrets of writing.*)

Be especially cautious if you're asking someone from a marginalized community to do you a favor for free. If you want feedback on how you've represented a culture, get a paid sensitivity read. Don't ask people from marginalized communities to give you permission to write about their culture.

I'm not someone who finds it easy to ask for help. I don't like feeling obligated to others. It's also easy to let my pride get in the way of asking for help. When I told one of my Iranian co-workers that I was planning to visit Iran, she told me her family would be happy to help if I had any issues. She warned me it was difficult for foreigners to get cash when they were in Iran (due to economic sanctions, Visa and Mastercard aren't available). I'm an experienced traveler and I made preparations to take extra cash. Due to a series of events (including the single ATM in Istanbul airport's departures lounge being out of order), I didn't have nearly enough cash when I arrived, but was reluctant to ask my co-worker's family for help. I didn't want to impose and felt embarrassed about letting myself get into that situation. I didn't want to cut short my trip, so I reached out to my co-worker's family. At short notice, they loaned me a substantial amount of cash, invited me to stay in their apartment and took me around the sights of Tehran. Their kindness was one of the highlights of my travels.

When people help you, make the effort to at least send them a personalized thank you. Look out for opportunities to help them.

There's a difference between asking someone for a favor and following up when someone owes you something. When an agent or editor has said they'll get back to you with a response by a certain date and that date has passed, don't feel bad about sending a polite message asking for an update. Especially when you're dealing with magazines, there will be times when you have to chase up publishers to get paid. No one likes having to act like a debt collection agency. It can be especially awkward if you're friends with the publisher. You deserve to be paid for your work. If you've tried to resolve this and are still waiting for your payment, one option is to enlist the aid of a professional organization. For example, SFWA has a grievance committee which can contact the publisher on your behalf.

Although it can make you feel uncomfortable, developing the ability to ask for help is important. It can be difficult to get the balance right between being asking for help and being overly demanding (and people have their own views on where this line is drawn), but people who are able to call on help from others are more likely to succeed.

SAYING NO

Invest in a piece of jewellery or a piece of art that is just the word NO. Wear it when you're working—or hang it where you can see it while you sit down to answer email.
- Kelly Link

Just as it's important to ask for help, you also need to be able to say no. Sometimes this means disappointing friends and missing out on exciting opportunities, but you can't do everything. After you've worked so hard, it can feel wrong to turn down an opportunity. Sometimes overcommitting can spur you on to greater productivity, but it can also cause stress and misery. It can be thrilling the first time an editor personally invites you to contribute, but eventually there comes a point when you don't have time for all the projects. There might be a voice telling you that you should never miss an opportunity and that if you say no, no one will invite you to do anything ever again. But you need to prioritize what's best for your career. Sometimes this means saying no.

The more well-known you become, the more strangers will ask you to read their stories or to give them advice. *How do I learn how to write short stories?* Yes, it's great to help people. Mentor people when you have the chance. But sometimes you need to say no. Your time is precious. If your book is a bestseller, you wouldn't have time to do your own writing if you gave everyone detailed personal replies. The *FAQ* is your friend. Instead of answering the same question over and over again, direct people to a page on your web site.

There are also situations where you definitely want to say no. Publishers who are making a profit, but who don't have any money to pay the writer. Exploitative contracts asking for all your rights.

Saying no can be difficult when you're offered something you've been working for years to achieve, but it isn't quite right. You've dreamed of having an agent and get an offer from an agent who might not be quite right for you. A bad agent is worse than no agent and can derail your career. Even a good agent might not be the right fit for you. Sometimes you might get multiple offers from agents and you're going to have to say no to some of them. This is never an easy decision, but you should be guided by who you think will be best for your career (of course this is difficult to tell when you've only briefly spoke to someone). Reach out to the agents' other clients and ask how their relationship works.

You might get an offer from a publisher and the deal isn't what you wanted (assuming you have reasonable expectations!). Hopefully you have an agent who is acting in your best interests and can give you honest advice about what to do.

Being able to say no to yourself is also important. Sometimes you should allow yourself not to do something. Sometimes you need to be able to take a break.

LIVING WITH SOMEONE WHO DOESN'T RESPECT YOUR WRITING

Having a partner who doesn't respect your writing is one of the hardest situations to deal with. You can try to make things better with improved communication, but ultimately it comes down to giving up your writing, shielding your writing from them, or relying on them to change. It can also be difficult if your parents are dismissive of your writing. They might urge you to forget about that silly hobby and get a real job. At least with your parents it will be easier to shield that part of your life from them. It can hurt not to share your writing success, but that can be better than letting them diminish your happiness.

With a partner you're living with, it's much harder not to share your writing life. There are different levels of support a partner can give. They might not be interested in reading your stories (I think it's best not to push people who don't have an interest in reading a particular genre), but they can still support and encourage your writing by treating your time with respect and by celebrating your successes. Jeff VanderMeer's *Booklife* discusses these scenarios and I'd recommend reading that if it's an issue you're dealing with.

Maybe your partner is indifferent to your writing and doesn't understand why you're so excited about getting a personal rejection from a magazine. You wish they'd take more of an interest in your writing, but maybe they have activities you don't get excited about either. It all depends on your relationship and what suits you both.

Maybe your partner wants you to be happy, but they resent how much time you spend on writing. Sometimes this can be an attempt to control you, sometimes this can be that they have a different ideal balance between spending time alone versus with their partner. Maybe they don't like you going to conventions and are jealous of the time you spend with your writing friends. These are things you're going to have to negotiate with your partner. Some people like the idea of having a partner who writes (*You're so creative!*), but don't want to give you time to write.

It's a serious problem if your partner's actively hostile to your writing. Maybe they tell you you're wasting your time and you should quit. This often means it's time to be thinking about why you're in a relationship with someone who doesn't support you or respect what's important to you. Sometimes you want to stay with your partner, you just want them to be kinder and more understanding. This might mean going to counseling, but ultimately you're relying on them to change. Maybe you have to close off that part of your life from them and write while they're out. Try writing at a cafe instead of at home. If you have writing friends facing similar problems, sharing your issues with them might make you feel better.

Having a partner who is a writer too can seem to be the ideal scenario. They are your insightful first reader, give you time to write and are your number one cheerleader. It can be wonderful to be in a relationship with another writer, but it doesn't always work this way. Maybe your career takes off and your partner is getting nothing but rejections and starts to blame you for holding back their career. Jealousy between writing spouses can be difficult to handle.

NETWORKING FOR MISANTHROPES

My lifetime dream is to be sitting at the bottom of a well.
  - Haruki Murakami

One of the most powerful things I ever did for my career, and my continued sanity, was to get to know other writers facing the same challenges. Social networks like Twitter and Facebook, supplemented with the occasional convention, have connected me with incredible people willing to share their own fraught publishing journeys. What stunned me more than anything else is how each of us thought our experiences were entirely unique, when it turned out we shared many of the same fears and frustrations.
  - Kameron Hurley

When I feel bad about my social skills I remind myself how one time Rachmaninoff decided he was gonna be pals with Stravinsky (who'd casually mentioned he liked honey) so he showed up at his house in the middle of the night with an enormous jar of honey and no explanation.
  - Iris Kaye-Smith

Many people hate the idea of networking. If you frame networking as the chance to spend time with people with similar interests, it becomes more palatable. While it's possible to succeed as a writer if you don't have any writing friends, it's a lot harder. You're missing out on a support network of people who can encourage and support you when you encounter setbacks.

In *Big Potential*, Shawn Achor writes about studies showing that social connections are usually a better indicator of success at university than SAT scores. Does that mean the world is inherently unfair and it's all about who you know? Not always, but having friends who are writers is one of the best things you can do for your career. A 2018 research paper by Paul Ingram and Mitali Banerjee examined the success of early twentieth century artists and concluded that a strong network of friends was a better predictor of an artist's success than artistic talent. Obviously there are different criteria for judging artistic success, but widening your circle of friends can have many benefits.

As well as providing support and opportunities, having friends by your side can even influence your view of the world in surprising ways. Achor writes that "Researchers found that if you are looking at a hill and judging how steep it is, the mere presence of social support around you transforms your perception. In fact, if you look at a hill while standing next to someone you consider to be a friend, the hill looks 10 to 20 percent less steep than if you were facing the hill alone. That is a stunning finding. Perception of your objective, physical world is transformed by including others in your pursuit of achievement."

Another benefit of writing friends is that hanging out with other writers and talking about writing can reinforce your identity as a writer. It can also increase the enjoyment you derive from writing success—sharing your publication news with people who understand the difficulty of the process can help you appreciate it more.

I'm generally a quiet person. I'd rather listen to what others have to say and it takes me a while to get to know people. Traveling and staying in youth hostels helped me become more comfortable with meeting people. My parents are both more social than me. My mother grew up in a country town and was used to knowing everyone. When I was in primary (elementary) school, at the end of the school year, my mother would invite my teacher over to our house for afternoon tea. When I got my first full-time job I made sure to regularly visit the other departments and chat with people to see how they were going. I used to think it was strange that other people didn't do the same thing. As I've got older, it's harder to keep doing these things. It's easier to fall into the trap of being less curious and interested in meeting people. I already have my friends, why do I need to meet more people? At work there's always something to do. I don't have as much time for general chit-chat. I have to remind myself to make more of an effort to be social. I enjoy spending time with my friends, but I also enjoy doing things by myself. It's important to get the balance right.

I have friends all over the world, which is great, but it's harder to maintain close friendships when you're in different countries. Especially when your friends get married and have children. When I returned to Melbourne after living overseas for five years, I didn't have that many friends in Melbourne any more. I made a deliberate effort to expand my social networks. I attended local genre conventions. I joined a couple of book clubs and a board games group through meetup.com and met some of my closest friends that way.

What if going to social events makes you anxious and you're terrified of making a social gaffe online? What if you live in a rural area and don't live near any other writers?

Many cities have writing meetup groups. Nanowrimo allows you to connect with other writers online and many cities have Nanowrimo events. If you attend a multi-week writing workshop, hopefully you'll make friends there.

Conventions can be a good way to make writing friends, but what if you don't know anyone? The first couple of conventions I went to, I listened to the panels and then went home. I don't drink alcohol and the idea of hanging around a crowded bar where I didn't know anyone wasn't appealing. I much prefer talking to a small group of friends than trying to join in noisy bar conversations. Genre conventions can feel like awfully cliquey places—all the famous people are hanging out together and no one invites you to join in. Often it's not that people are deliberately excluding you, it might be the only chance they have to catch up with friends they only see once a year.

I find the idea of going to a convention where I don't know anyone less intimidating than one where I know a few people, but none of them very well. If I don't know anyone, I don't feel any social obligations to mingle. I don't feel bad about listening to panels and going home. I've been to conventions where there were awkward meetings with people I'd met a couple of times before but who never remembered who I was. I'm comfortable talking with people one-on-one, but I find mingling at parties awkward. If you're shy it can take a while to make friends, but most conventions have areas where it can be easier to have a conversation than at a noisy bar. If you're lucky enough to be able to attend a convention with a more well-connected friend, ask them to introduce you to other people.

I suspect that one of the reasons I'm a computer programmer, that I love board games, that I worked as a teacher, and that I enjoyed school is that I feel comfortable when there are rules about how things are supposed to work. If you're someone who likes a framework upon which to base social interactions, you could try making your own rules to encourage yourself to be more social. *You have to talk to someone new every day. You have to talk to someone wearing red today.*

One of the best ways I've found of making friends at conventions is to be on panels together. It's a good way to meet new people and discover shared interests. Of course being on a panel can make some people anxious. Why would anyone listen to you talk about a subject when there are people who know much more about it? If you feel like you don't have enough experience, look out for panel topics revolving around discussions of your favorite books or shows. At some of the bigger conventions like World-con, there are more people applying to be on panels than there is space for panelists, so try not to be disappointed if you don't get offered a place. Applying for panels can be particularly fraught for people from marginalized communities. There are examples of conventions excluding award nominees because they weren't *famous enough* and sometimes the only panel you'll be offered is the *Diversity 101* panel. The situation is slowly improving, but if you're unsure about how seriously the programming committee takes issues of representation and diversity, ask your friends for advice. The same applies for accessibility issues. Conventions that claim they are accessible sometimes don't even ensure there's a ramp to get to the speakers' stage.

It can help to prepare a brief outline of things you want to mention during the panel. Make sure you use the microphone and try not to speak too quickly. Don't be the guy who interrupts the other panelists. Don't turn the panel into a sales pitch for your book. There's a good chance someone will ask you for recommendations of books or stories covering the panel's topic. Think of a few recommendations beforehand. Make sure not all of your recommendations are written by older white guys.

There are also safety issues to consider. There are plenty of examples of well-known writers and editors behaving inappropriately or worse. Make sure the convention has an anti-harassment policy and check for reports of how seriously complaints are taken.

Try not to make others uncomfortable and be wary of

intruding on private conversations or making comments on people's appearance. Don't be that guy!

If you find yourself talking to a famous author or an editor, don't ask them to read your book. If they want to read it, they'll let you know. If you're working on a book, have a short answer prepared for when people ask what your book's about.

Be kind to people.

Be respectful of people's pronouns. If you get someone's pronoun wrong, don't make a big deal of it. Apologize and move on. Don't start avoiding someone because you got their pronouns wrong. (This happens!)

Show an interest in other people. Don't tell someone they're stupid for liking a particular show or book. Don't badmouth entire genres. It's great to be passionate about your favorite books and movies, but don't tell someone you can't believe they haven't watched a particular movie or read a particular book. Do you know how many books are published each year? No one can read them all. Don't look down on younger people who haven't read what you consider *the classics*. Many older books are full of sexism and racism. Science fiction in particular, often doesn't age well. (Of course that doesn't mean you should only read new books).

If you meet someone from another country, be wary of making the boring, obvious, or obnoxious comments about their country. If you meet someone from Colombia, rethink your life choices if your instinct is to make a joke about drug dealers. If you meet someone from Sweden, don't immediately tell them you've been to Norway. Don't assume foreigners grew up in poverty. Don't assume you know where someone is from—most Chinese people won't be pleased if you assume they're Japanese. The Australian Prime Minister recently made headlines when he greeted a Korean woman by saying *ni hao*.

Don't assume someone is a foreigner just because they're not white. Avoid complimenting people on how well they speak English. In most cases it comes across as patronizing. Imitating foreign accents isn't as nearly as funny as a lot of people seem to think it is. It makes me wince when international guest speakers try to ingratiate themselves with an Australian audience by saying *g'day* in a faux-Australian accent. (And that's even without the dose of racism that accompanies imitating accents from some countries).

It can be hard to remember people's names and if you're unsure, ask. Don't tell people that their names are unpronounceable.

Don't tell people you don't see color.

Don't try too hard to prove your woke credentials to people from marginalized communities.

Don't hug or touch people unless you know they're comfortable with it.

Don't ask physically disabled people how they manage to have sex.

Don't ask women when they're going to have children.

If someone says they don't drink alcohol, don't tell them that one drink won't hurt.

Be cautious about offering *silver lining* advice. *Well, at least the crocodile didn't eat both of your parents.*

If you possess powers of smartassery, use them for good instead of evil.

Avoid *for a* praise. *You know a lot about science fiction for a woman.*

If you're in a group, give people the opportunity to join in your conversation (but don't assume everyone wants to —they might be waiting to meet friends).

Don't schedule too many activities. Make sure you include time to rest and recharge.

What if you have online friends who are going to be at

the same convention? Should you arrange a time to meet up beforehand? Or is it better not to schedule too many things and catch up with people when you run into them in the bar? That all depends on the size of the convention (at some of the bigger conventions you can miss seeing people all together), how much you want to meet them and how busy your schedules are. It can feel awkward asking someone to take the time to meet you, especially if they're more well-known than you. In most cases it's good to ask— people want to meet friends they've talked to online, but don't be disappointed if they don't have the time. They may have editors and agents they have to organize meetings with. If you're a man inviting a woman to meet up, be cautious how you do it—you may be forcing someone to evaluate whether they're being asked to meet a friend or are being asked on a date.

If you find yourself with too many people you want to meet, try scheduling a time at a bar or cafe and tell people you'll be there at a certain time if they want to catch up with you.

If you meet people at a convention and enjoy talking to them, reach out after the convention to let them know you enjoyed meeting them.

Of course not everyone has the opportunity to attend conventions or workshops. There are plenty of ways to get to know other writers online. There are writing organizations like *The Science Fiction and Fantasy Writers of America* (SFWA) or *The Romance Writers of America* (RWA) and similar organizations in other countries. Look for online forums for writers. I've made a lot of friends through the Codex forum. You can also make friends with other writers on online groups dedicated to particular shows or books with big fan bases. You can join discussions about writing on Twitter. Even though people are having public conversations, that doesn't always mean your opinion is welcome, especially if it's a negative one. Don't join in an online conversation to tell people how stupid they are for liking their favorite movie.

I've made friends in other countries via a postcard exchange web site, and had the chance to visit them in person when I went to their country.

If you have an agent, reach out to the other writers your agent represents. If you're in an anthology, try to get to know the other writers in the book—especially if you have the chance to meet them at the launch.

Another way of making more connections is being known as an expert in a non-writing field. Maybe you're the person people go to when they want to know about AI, or plane crashes, or Japanese history.

Try not to feel anxious about online personal branding. The most important part of any writing career is determining the suffix of the adjective applied to writing in your style. If someone reads a book about a bear detective solving mysteries in the village do I want them to view it as Doylesque or Doyleian?

Don't worry if you only have a few online followers. It's much better to make a few friends online than artificially inflating your follower count by following as many people as you can in the hope they'll follow back. Yes, it can be depressing when you make a joke and no one notices and then a month later someone else makes the same joke and gets a billion retweets and a Nobel Prize.

If you've had a story published, make sure you have a way for people to contact you. It can simply be a static web site with a link to your story and your contact details. You don't want to make it difficult for editors to contact you if they want to reprint your work.

Be wary of offering unsolicited advice, especially when it comes to health issues. The chances are you don't know the full circumstances and they've already considered the obvious options. If people are asking for recommendations for books or stories from people of color, don't be the one who recommends books by older white guys with the explanation that you don't see color.

Volunteering is another way to make friends. Genre magazines are often on the lookout for slush readers. I've been reading stories for *PodCastle* for a couple of years and I've made friends that way.

Sometimes it can feel like you have a lot of online acquaintances, but few real friends. There are people who congratulate when you have a story accepted, but they aren't really part of your life. The difference can feel especially sharp when you compare it to writers who have formed close friendships at a writing workshop and are now loving on each other online. Sometimes it takes time for people to get to know you. Being public in your love of something can be a good way to make friends. I have a group of friends, *The Pastry Crew*, with whom I share photos of cakes and donuts.

Make an effort to congratulate others on their achievements and let them know when you've enjoyed reading their stories. Sometimes you don't want to come across as too much of a *fan* and you want to let them know you're a serious writer too, so you tell them a few things you loved about their book, as well as one thing you think they could have improved. That way they will acknowledge you as a peer. Don't do that. If you write, *This was the best book I ever read. It changed my life. The ending could have been better,* which part do you think most authors will focus on? Don't contact people to give them negative opinions.

If your friendships are based around activities—friends from a book club—and you stop the activity, it's easy for the friendships to fade away. With social media it's easier to stay in contact, but it's likely you'll need to put in extra effort to maintain friendships where you no longer regularly see the person. One way is to put aside a time each week and send a message to a friend you haven't heard from in a while. Schedule a catchup session. It's nice to check how people are doing and let them know what you've been up to.

Making friends can be a slow process, but it's one of the best things you can do for your writing career and for your happiness.

THE IMPORTANCE OF BEING KIND

People will forget what you said or what you did, but they will never forget how you made them feel.
  - *Maya Angelou*

You should be kind to other people, even if it's only for selfish reasons. It's one of the best ways to feel good about yourself. It helps strengthen your friendships. If you are kind to people, they're more likely to help you when you need it.

Being kind to other people doesn't mean you have to tolerate hateful people. You don't to agree with everyone's point of view or make time for everyone. Block and mute people on social media if they annoy you.

When you have the chance, help people. Especially if you're in a position of power. Look for opportunities to mentor other writers. Mention market opportunities to others. One of the best ways you can help people is by connecting other writers. If you're at a convention, introduce different groups of friends to each other.

Make sure people actually want your help though. Too many books on happiness come across as patronizing when they recommend helping *old people* and *disabled people*. Not everyone wants your help.

Avoid patronizing *compliments*. Don't tell disabled people you've just met that you think they're brave.

If you're white, learn to recognize the white savior complex. Don't assume foreigners are worse off than people in your country.

Deriving Moral Superiority from Your Achievements is an easy trap to fall into. *I worked hard and I got published. You haven't been published, so that means you haven't worked hard.* What worked for you is dependent upon timing and your circumstances. If other writers are doing things differently, it doesn't necessarily mean they're doing them wrong.

Share what you've learned. (Without mansplaining). One of the best ways to learn a subject is to explain it to someone else.

If you're in a critique group, be kind with your feedback. Avoid the temptation to make grandiose statements that you think make you sound clever. *Worst. Story. Ever* kind of comments. That doesn't mean you have to be dishonest in your praise, but avoid being cruel.

Go to your friends' book launches. Buy your friends cake to celebrate their success.

FAILURE

THE TRY FAIL CYCLE

TEN THINGS I LEARNED FROM FAILURE

Kameron Hurley

Kameron Hurley is an award-winning author who grew up in Washington State, and has lived in Fairbanks, Alaska; Durban, South Africa; and Chicago. She has a degree in historical studies from the University of Alaska and a Master's in History from the University of KwaZulu-Natal, specializing in the history of South African resistance movements. Her essay on the history of women in conflict "We Have Always Fought" was the first essay to win a Hugo Award.

This essay was originally published in Female First.

You're going to fail the first couple times through.

I've been writing novels for more than a decade, and every single one of those novels was a complete failure the first time I wrote it. Novel writing, like so many things in life, is an iterative process. You come at it again and again, working at it like you would a piece of pottery or a stone sculpture, chipping away the parts that don't make sense, smoothing over the rough edges. But we all start with the lump of clay, the formless gob, and there will be many moments along the way that the blob looks like an abject failure. It's persistence that makes it great.

Today's failure could be tomorrow's success.

I've failed a lot in my life, personally and professionally. The first few times you fail feel like your first big breakup: darkness comes down like a cloud, like the world has ended, and you don't believe you'll ever recover. When I pitched my latest novel, *The Stars are Legion*, to my agent back in 2013, she said it was going to be tough to sell a book with no men in it in genre like science fiction. I believed otherwise, but I was willing to wait for my moment. So, I put that pitch aside and we worked on something else. But while the novel sat, the market changed, and I had an editor call up looking for a space opera. Turns out I had one, and just like that – the book we didn't think could sell was hitting the shelves in hard-cover. There are no failed ideas, just ideas that haven't found their moment yet.

I don't fully understand something unless I fail at it.

Many people don't even want to start something until they feel fairly confident that they will be a success at it. But me? I love to throw myself into things headfirst and fail all over the place. I'm like this with learning languages, with painting, with writing. Mimicking others' work only takes you so far. I have to make my own mistakes before I figure out how to do something right.

Failing can be fun.

Lots of folks say you have to "give permission" to your-self to fail, like it's something that needs to be excused. But failing when the stakes are pretty low can actually be fun. I've written experimental flash fiction that failed hard, but had a blast doing it.

Giving up benefits your enemies.

Your enemies love your failures, sure. But what they love even more is to see you brought so low by those fail-ures that you never get up again. Sometimes enemies aren't even external. Often, our biggest critic, our greatest enemy, is ourselves. There's a great satisfaction in proving that part of us wrong.

You mean more to the people in your life than you imagine.

I moved out of my house when I was 19 and tried to make it on my own. I failed. I had to call up my parents and ask them for help. It was one of the hardest things I'd done up until that point, and I wasn't confident they would help. It was so difficult to ask for help that I legitimately considered offing myself as an alternative, because then I wouldn't have to live with that failure! How awful is that? My parents had demanded success, and back then I thought success meant everything. I was wrong. Long-term success means learning how to live with failure.

Drugs aren't so bad.

During the launch of my fifth book, I hit a wall of fear and anxiety that threatened to undo everything I'd built toward in my career. I was failing to turn in work on time, pushing out writing deadlines, and ultimately, failing to create new work. That failure taught me that it was time to seek out a solution. I reached out to my doctor and got some prescription help for the anxiety that made it possible for me to work again – and work better. I also changed my work habits to ensure I didn't have a breakdown like that again. Failure can teach you what your limits are.

Embrace happy accidents.

Writing used to be a passion project for me, but over the last decade or so, it's become a profession. I no longer had a low-stakes hobby to invest myself in anymore where failure cost me nothing. That's where Bob Ross, the painter on PBS, came in. The 29 seasons of his soothing how-to-paint programs are all up on Netflix, and now I chill out at night at my canvas painting truly awful paintings. Really awful! But perfection isn't the point, as Ross reminds viewers. As he notes, "There are no mistakes. Only happy accidents." Messed up a tree? Turn it into a rock. Made a bad stroke in that mountain? Paint a tree over it. And you know what? It turns out that sometimes the stuff you create out of the accident is better than what you would have had otherwise.

Losing can be more motivating than winning.

I've lost my share of big awards and big opportunities. I've also won my share of the same. But when it comes to what motivates me most in life, it's not the big wins that inspire me to push harder, do more, be better. It's the losses. The losses remind me of what I still have to reach for; what's still worth fighting for.

Failing is better than giving up.

There's an old proverb, "Fall down seven times. Get up eight." The secret to success in life isn't to avoid falling down. The secret is in being able to get up again, and again, and again, until the day your mortality catches up to you. The most important thing I ever learned from failure was how to get up again, and live to fight another day.

WHEN THINGS GO WRONG

If tacos can fall apart and still be delicious and worthy of love, so can you.
   - R.M. Moore

Even when you think you've succeeded, things will inevitably go wrong. This doesn't mean you should feel anxious about every negative possibility, but it helps to at least be mentally prepared for some of the things that might go wrong. Finding the right balance between preparation and hoping for the best is difficult but important. The trick is not to make yourself anxious or pessimistic. Instead, think of it as a fire drill. The people who respond first in an emergency are often not the bravest ones, they're the ones who have thought about what they would do if that situation happened. I did a weekend parachuting course and we practiced over and over again what to do if our chute got tangled and didn't properly open. The chances of it happening are small, but if it does, you want to be able to respond by reflex. It's extremely unlikely that writing is going to put you in a life or death situation, but there are situations where people panic and don't think through the consequences of their actions. They say the wrong thing on social media and instead of apologizing, they become defensive and make things worse.

Your story is accepted and then the magazine folds before it publishes it. Having an acceptance turn into nothing can be particularly heartbreaking. It can be worse if it happens with a novel and a publisher.

You get a three-book contract and then your first novel sales are disappointing and the publisher cancels the contract.

Your editor changes publishing houses and your new editor isn't enthusiastic about the series.

Sometimes things happen that no one could have anticipated. Jeff VanderMeer writes "I've also had to pull a book because the editor became a born-again Christian and wanted my characters to correspond to figures in the Bible."

Nicole Bross' debut novel was somehow misclassified on Amazon and listed as a pair of shorts. When the author tried ordering her own book, she got a pair of shorts instead.

Things can go wrong with the publication itself. I've had short stories and award nominations where my name has been spelled wrong. Podcasts can mispronounce your name. A publisher can get your pronouns wrong. There have even been instances of publishers altering a bio to use different pronouns.

Sometimes files will get messed up and they'll publish the uncorrected version of the story. Mistakes in your first publication can feel particularly cruel. You want to show it to all your friends, but your name is spelled wrong. In most cases online publications will quickly correct the mistake if you let them know.

Your agent drops you because they can't sell your books. After publishers rejected my novel, my first agent dropped me to concentrate on her bestselling clients. This felt awful and killed my enthusiasm for writing for a long time.

Your agent loses enthusiasm for your work. They start taking forever to reply to your questions. You realize your agent isn't helping your career and it's better to part ways. This is never an easy decision to make. It can feel like you're going backwards. You had an agent, and now you're on your own. It's much better to have no agent than to have a wrong agent though.

After your story's been published someone will point out the historical details you got wrong. Or you will get names and dates wrong in a non-fiction book. It's important to pay close attention to details (especially people's names!), but inevitably you're going to make a mistake. You can add an online errata to your web site and have it corrected in the next edition. It's not the end of the world.

Books have been pulled from publication after early reviewers noticed problematic elements. This would be a devastating thing to happen. Taking care to research your work, considering if you're the right person to tell the story, and using sensitivity readers can reduce the chances of this happening.

You might hate your book's cover. Don't publicly make fun of the artist because you think it's a bad illustration (yes, at least one author has done this). Raise the issue with your agent and editor. You don't often get to choose the cover, but if a publisher knows you hate the cover, they might consider changing it. Sometimes publishers white-wash covers—the main characters are magically transformed into white people when they appear on the book's cover. How much should you protest? That depends on you, what you believe is important, and whether you'd be proud to show the book to your friends.

Most famous writers have a story about no one turning up to their book signing.

Silicon Valley makes a big deal about learning from failure. *Fail fast. Fail often.* There's even a tech conference called *FailCon* based around the idea of learning from failure. It's important to consider who has the privilege of being allowed to fail. Entrepreneurs urging people to embrace failure usually have another means of financial support. By all means, follow your dreams, but be cautious about quitting your day job to become a full-time writer. Writers are vulnerable to uneven income streams.

So what do you do when things go wrong? It helps if you don't feel alone. Reach out to the people who should be supporting you—your agent, your editor, your writing friends. When Kate Heartfield's first novel *Armed in Her Fashion* was published, the first print edition had a page missing which contained a major plot point. Kate describes how she dealt with the situation.

"What made me feel better about it was: my agent and my publisher were both immediately on it, and took it seriously, and worked to fix it. It was around 10 p.m. in our time zone when we all became aware of it (because someone mentioned it on Twitter) and the emails were flying as we all worked to get to the bottom of it and figure out how we were going to make it right. That made me feel that I was not alone. It made me feel better that this was a mistake that crept in at the very last stage before printing, after we'd proofed it. It wasn't careless proofreading. My publisher quickly worked with the distributor and came up with a plan to include inserts for the bookstore copies, and stickers for the ones they sell themselves at conventions. I had, meanwhile, put a pdf of the page up at my website and offered to mail signed copies of the page to anyone who wanted one. My thinking was really informed by Mary Robinette Kowal's example of how she had dealt with a missing first sentence: Get on top of it, communicate with readers, and do everything you can to make it up to them. Readers have been wonderful about it. Nobody's got mad at me or complained. A couple of readers have been really appreciative of the mailed, signed pages I sent them. One reader painstakingly filled in the missing text by hand, which is so lovely. So it really is a collector's edition, although I'd still rather it had been intact in the first place.

There was also one thing that made me feel worse: The day I got my author copies, just as I was unboxing them to the sound of angelic trumpets (in my head, anyway), my mom flipped through one and mentioned something about a blank page. I was so unwilling to let anything spoil the unboxing of my very first novel, that moment I'd been dreaming of for so many years, that I went into denial mode and assumed it was just a bit of odd formatting she was seeing, not actual missing text, and I dismissed it with a 'well, there's nothing we can do about that now.' I should have looked more closely, realized then that the page was actually missing, and set about fixing it then, instead of days later when the comment on Twitter made me realize there was text missing. So the lesson is: It's better to have your happiness ruined in the moment than to let something slip by that could cause bigger problems. Also, always listen to your mother."

KNOWING WHEN TO QUIT

Quitting is not giving up, it's choosing to focus your attention on something more important. Quitting is not losing confidence, it's realizing that there are more valuable ways you can spend your time. Quitting is not making excuses, it's learning to be more productive, efficient and effective instead. Quitting is letting go of things (or people) that are sucking the life out of you so you can do more things that will bring you strength.

   - Osayi Osar-Emokpae

Knowing when to quit is an underrated skill. If something isn't right for you, then in most cases, the earlier you quit, the better. Everyone quits lots of things. No one has the time to do everything. Books you'll never read. Places you'll never visit. Stories you'll never write.

Romantic comedies have helped spread the idea that if someone tells you they're not interested in dating you, the correct response is to keep pursuing them. Sometimes the real world differs from fiction.

In *Big Potential,* Shawn Achor writes "Perseverance and grit, while critically important, are not always the best course of action... When we persist for too long at certain goals... it can, at times, come at the expense of our accomplishing others... Quitters sometimes DO win. Defence, resilience, and grit are valuable, but only to a point."

The *sunk cost fallacy* is when people keep pouring more resources into a project because they don't want to lose the resources they've already spent, but the smart thing would be to quit.

What about the question of whether you should quit writing? You've tried to get a book published, but you've got nothing but rejections. You have to evaluate what's best for you. If you write for fifty years and never get published will that make you happier than if you quit after a year? Many writers who *succeed* and get a book published have to deal with disappointing sales and a lack of critical acclaim. Most writers don't hit the bestseller lists. Most writers don't earn enough to make a living from their writing income. Is that still worth the effort for you?

Sometimes giving up is the right decision. Maybe you will save yourself years of heartache. Maybe you'd kind of like to be a writer, but there are other things which will make you happier. If you just want to get something published, you can self-publish a book and move onto something else.

What if you're tempted to quit because you think you'll never make it? There are uncountable examples of writers who struggled in obscurity for years before finding success. Award-winning Australian writer, Elizabeth Jolley started writing in her twenties, but her first book wasn't published until she was fifty-three. She went on to publish fifteen novels.

Another thing is to adjust your expectations. Being a writer doesn't mean you have to earn your living as a writer. You can keep your day job and write in your spare time.

What if you're clinging to the dream of being a full-time writer, but are burned out? Work out the best way to recharge your energy. Take a break and try again. Go to a writing workshop to get some inspiration. Reread your favorite book. Read a book you hate and vow to write something better. Write fan fiction for your favorite show. Watch TED talks for inspiration.

Beware of people who give toxic advice such as *Anyone who can be persuaded to quit isn't a real writer*.

People's circumstances change. Deciding to take a break from writing doesn't have to be a final decision.

Plenty of writers put their writing on hold at various times. I never considered quitting, but I didn't write any fiction for a couple of years after I moved to Japan. Adjusting to life in a new country was a higher priority for me at the time.

Sometimes people achieve all they want when it comes to writing. They had a story published. They don't feel the need to keep writing and that's fine.

If you take joy in the writing process itself, it can be easier to sustain a long career. Sometimes it's worth persevering through all of the disappointment. Your book gets published and you get a fan letter that means the world. My first short story was professionally published in 1993. Seventeen years later I received my first award nomination for one of my short stories.

What about quitting individual novels? When is it the right decision to abandon an unfinished book? Again, this depends on the individual circumstances. Sometimes you know there are serious flaws and a book's not worth pursuing. There is a value in finishing something though. Especially if it's your first novel. It can be worth the effort to prove to yourself that you're able to finish a book. If you keep abandoning books because your writing has improved and you know you're capable of better, you might never end up finishing a book. A first draft doesn't need to be perfect. That's what revision is for. It's also important to remember that many writers initially think their stories are awful. In *On Writing*, Stephen King mentions how thought his opening for *Carrie* was terrible and he threw the pages in the waste-basket. "I couldn't see wasting two weeks, maybe even a month, creating a novella I didn't like and wouldn't be able to sell. So I threw it away." His wife retrieved the pages and convinced him to continue with the story. *Carrie* eventually became his first published book.

THE 9 AND 3/4 PLATFORMS OF REJECTION

The book is so endlessly complicated by details of reference and information, the interim legends become so much of a nuisance despite their relevance, that the very action of the story seems to be to become hopelessly bogged down and the book, eventually, unreadable. The whole is so dry and airless, so lacking in pace, that whatever drama and excitement the novel might have had is entirely dissipated by what does seem, a great deal of the time, to be extraneous material. My thanks nonetheless for having thought of us. The manuscript of The Left Hand of Darkness *is returned herewith.*
  - Rejection letter sent to Ursula K. Le Guin

The best reaction to a rejection slip is a sort of wild-eyed madness, an evil grin, and sitting yourself in front of the keyboard muttering 'Okay, you bastards. Try rejecting this!' and then writing something so unbelievably brilliant that all other writers will disembowel themselves with their pens upon reading it, because there's nothing left to write. Because the rejection slips will arrive. And, if the books are published, then you can pretty much guarantee that bad reviews will be as well. And you'll need to learn how to shrug and keep going.
  - Neil Gaiman

Countless bestsellers and classics work of literature were initially rejected by publishers. A dozen publishers rejected the first Harry Potter book. *Dune, Anne Frank's Diary, Gone With the Wind, The Catcher in the Rye* weren't good enough for some publishers.

If you're a writer, you have to deal with rejection. Sometimes it's because the publisher doesn't understand the market. Sometimes it's because they don't understand the book. Sometimes it's because they've already bought a book with a similar theme.

Some writers practice the art of *rejectomancy*—trying to determine how likely a story is to be accepted based on how long the response is taking. Some writers put a lot of stock in whether they receive a form or a personal rejection and evaluate their story's worth from editorial comments. Generally that's a bad idea. While it can be a positive thing to get a personal rejection (this often means the editor saw something worth encouraging), don't equate your story's worth with whether you received a personal rejection. In my work as an editor sometimes it's easier to give a personal comment to a story because (for me) there's an obvious flaw that stands out, whereas it's harder to make comments on a story I might feel is stronger, but doesn't grab me enough to accept. It also depends on timing— towards the end of the submission deadline for *Sword and Sonnet* there were more stories to read, so I was less likely to send a personal rejection. When you're submitting to a magazine which has lots of slush readers, some of them might write personal rejections, whereas others are less inclined.

It can be disappointing when you've received a hold or a bump notice and then you get a form rejection. Again, this often means there's nothing obviously *wrong* with the story, but just that there are other stories the editor liked more.

Personal rejections where the editor tells you the story was close but didn't make the final cut, can be both encouraging and heartbreaking. These are often the hardest to deal with, especially for stories which earn multiple of these.

Don't write back and argue with an editor about a rejection. It's not going to change their mind and they're only going to think you're a difficult writer to work with.

Definitely don't write back and tell them your story was better than anything else they published. If you sell the story elsewhere, don't write to the editor who rejected the story to let them know how wrong they were. Magazines often have particular tastes—even knowing a story was going to win many awards, some editors would still reject it because it doesn't fit the kind of the stories they publish.

Don't post comments online about how stupid the magazine is for rejecting your story. (If a magazine tells you your story is *too full of the gay*, it can be appropriate to warn other writers they might want to avoid this market.

Should you write back and thank an editor for a helpful personal rejection? That depends on the magazine. Some magazines explicitly ask that you don't do this, it only gives them more to read. Other editors say they appreciate hearing how their feedback was useful. One solution is to send the magazine another submission and mention you found the comments helpful in your cover letter.

Should you revise a story based on comments in a rejection? Again, it depends on the circumstances. If you find the comments useful, revise the story before sending it out again. If the comments don't match what you want for the story, then ignore them. If five magazines send you rejections with comments about how the opening was too slow, then it's probably a good idea to edit the opening though.

What does the speed of the rejection tell you about the story's worth? Often nothing. Maybe the editor took longer than normal because they were busy or on vacation. Maybe the story got assigned to a slower slush reader. If you get a rejection back quickly (some magazines can respond in under an hour), it doesn't mean your story is extra bad. Rejoice that they didn't hold up your story and send it on to the next market. Editors don't need to read an entire story to know it's not right for them. More than half the time I can tell within the first couple of paragraphs that I'm going to reject a story.

If you have an agent and your book is out on submission, discuss with them how much of the gory details you want to know about what publishers are saying.

So how do you reduce the sting of rejection?

One of the best ways is to have lots of things out on submission. This reduces the pain of any one rejection. Obviously, this is easier if you're submitting short stories. Getting a rejection from a publisher because they don't think they can sell enough copies of your book is still going to hurt. Some short story writers aim for a certain number of submissions or rejections a year. Some of my friends tried a 100 rejections in a year challenge. This is a way of framing a rejection as being a step along the path to getting published. Three years I've managed to earn 100 rejections. They are also the three years I've sold the most stories. The more you submit, the more you're going to sell.

Another way is working out a submission plan for a story before you send it anywhere. Make a list of the top ten markets you want to send the story. When it comes back, you don't need to spend mental energy working out where to send it next. Simply submit it to the next market on the list. This can be complicated by markets that are only open for certain times of the year, but it's still a good process to follow.

It helps if you can separate your sense of self-worth from the story. This particular story was rejected by this particular magazine at this time. It doesn't mean you are a bad person. Although you generally shouldn't resubmit a story that has been previously rejected to the same magazine, there have been instances where a magazine got a new editor and they accepted stories the previous editor rejected.

It can be helpful to commiserate with your writing friends about rejections, particularly markets you were hopeful about. It can feel awful when you and a friend submit to the same anthology and their story is accepted and yours is rejected, but don't stomp on your friend's joy.

When Princeton professor Johannes Haushofer learned his friends were discouraged by missing out on jobs, he created a *CV of Failures*, a list of the jobs and grants he had applied for but been rejected. He wrote "Most of what I try fails, but these failures are often invisible, while the successes are visible. I have noticed that this sometimes gives others the impression that most things work out for me. As a result, they are more likely to attribute their own failures to themselves, rather than the fact that the world is stochastic, applications are crapshoots, and selection committees and referees have bad days. This CV of Failures is an attempt to balance the record and provide some perspective." People found his CV encouraging and he's made it available on his web site.

It can hurt when you're querying agents and you get nothing but rejections. It can feel like all that time you spent working on your book was wasted. Viewing the book as part of a learning process or a stepping stone can help, but often the best way is to derive pleasure from the act of creating something. If you can do this, you can be happy with writing itself, regardless of how the publishing part of things works out. For some people self-publishing is an alternative, but it's worth recognizing that your first writing will often be flawed and it can be worth putting it aside and beginning work on the next project. Even if you decide to trunk a novel, there's always the option of lifting parts of it to serve as inspiration for a future work.

MAKING YOUR OWN LUCK

When wealth is passed off as merit, bad luck is seen as bad character. This is how ideologues justify punishing the sick and the poor. But poverty is neither a crime nor a character flaw. Stigmatise those who let people die, not those who struggle to live.
  - Sarah Kendzior

In many domains people are tempted to think, after the fact, that an outcome was entirely predictable, and that the success of a musician, an actor, an author, or a politician was inevitable in light of his or her skills and characteristics. Beware of that temptation. Small interventions and even coincidences, at a key stage, can produce large variations in the outcome. Today's hot singer is probably indistinguishable from dozens and even hundreds of equally talented performers whose names you've never heard.
  - Richard H. Thaler

You'll hit gold more often if you simply try out a lot of things.
  - Ira Glass

If you reach the ranks of bestselling writers, it's natural to want to diminish the role that luck played in your glorious triumph. You worked hard. You were smarter than everyone else. You saw a market niche to be filled and responded with the right words. You did it all by yourself.

In reality, much of success is contingent upon circumstances outside of your control. A book in the same genre becomes a breakout hit and editors are looking for similar titles. A lot of what is described as *luck* is of course privilege. Your parents were wealthy and you went to a good school and a friend introduced you to their brother who was starting a new business. *You were lucky to get a good job.*

How do you make your own luck? Part of it is about showing up—making yourself available for opportunities. Part of it is helping other people. They will look out for opportunities for you. Making friends at workshops, conventions, and online is one of the best ways to increase your luck. The more social connections you have, the more opportunities will come your way. I've had stories published because I was friends with the editor and they had a sudden gap in their publication and didn't want to go through the work of an open submission period, so they asked me if I could send them a story. That doesn't mean my story only got published because of who I know, but the opportunity wouldn't have come my way otherwise. Especially when it comes to freelance articles for magazines, editors will often give preference to people they've worked with before. They want someone they know can deliver an article on time.

If you're in a position of power when it comes to accepting stories, it can be rewarding to help your friends, but make sure you also make the effort to reach out to others. You're going to be called out if you publish an anthology which only has white people in it. In IT and startups in particular, there's often an emphasis placed on whether a job candidate is a good *cultural fit* for the company. This is often used as a way of excluding marginalized people, yet studies show that diversity is good for business. Try to expand your social circle. (That doesn't mean you have to be friends with Nazis!)

Part of luck is anticipating obstacles and making preparations so you're not overwhelmed by bad events. Chris Hadfield talks about this in his book, *An Astronaut's Guide to Life on Earth*. "I'm not a nervous or pessimistic person. Really. If anything, I'm annoyingly upbeat, at least according to the experts (my family, of course). I tend to expect things will turn out well and they usually do. My optimism and confidence come not from feeling I'm luckier than other mortals, and they sure don't come from visualizing victory. They're the result of a lifetime spent visualizing defeat and figuring out how to prevent it. Like most astronauts, I'm pretty sure that I can deal with what life throws at me because I've thought about what to do if things go wrong, as well as right."

Things will go wrong that are outside of your control. Sales for your genre fall dramatically and no one's interested in buying your books. Your editor leaves your publishing house. Your publisher gets taken over and the new owners aren't interested in your kind of books. You can't anticipate all the possible scenarios, but thinking about the more common things that could go wrong can help you deal with them if they arise.

Another part of luck is being open to opportunities. Richard Wiseman is the author of *The Luck Factor* and talks about studies conducted on people who described themselves as especially lucky or unlucky. "We gave both lucky and unlucky people a newspaper, and asked them to look through it and tell me how many photographs were inside. On average, the unlucky people took about two minutes to count the photographs, whereas the lucky people took just seconds. Why? Because the second page of the newspaper contained the message: 'Stop counting. There are 43 photographs in this newspaper.' This message took up half of the page and was written in type that was more than 2 inches high. It was staring everyone straight in the face, but the unlucky people tended to miss it and the lucky people tended to spot it. For fun, I placed a second large message halfway through the newspaper: 'Stop counting. Tell the experimenter you have seen this and win £250.' Again, the unlucky people missed the opportunity because they were still too busy looking for photographs... Lucky people's ability to notice opportunities is a result of their relaxed way of looking at the world. It is not that they expect to find certain opportunities, but rather that they notice them when they come across them. In contrast, unlucky people tend to be more anxious. They are so busy counting the photographs they don't notice the advertisement... In real life, they might be focused on getting to a meeting on time, thinking about finding a new job or worrying about the problems in their lives. As a result, they have a very narrow, focused, beam of attention that can cause them to miss the unexpected opportunities that surround them on a daily basis."

Especially for writers, it's easy to be wrapped up in your own thoughts. When I'm walking to work, I'm often thinking about story ideas. When I'm traveling, I'm more open to exploring a new city and I notice more of my surroundings. Sometimes it can be useful not to be so focused on a single thing.

Wiseman says that lucky people make the most of chance opportunities. They pay attention to their intuition. They expect good fortune and they take practical steps to turn bad luck into good. Unlucky people tend to be more superstitious and are less inclined to take useful steps to solve the problem. He gives the example of someone who viewed themselves as jinxed because they'd had several car accidents. In contrast, someone who viewed themselves as lucky had several car accidents and so took driving lessons.

Thinking of yourself as lucky can be a self-fulfilling prophecy. If you expect good fortune, you apply for jobs. If you think people are likely to be friendly, you're friendlier to them. Wiseman did a survey where he asked people whether they viewed getting caught in a bank robbery and being shot in the arm as unlucky or lucky. The people who viewed themselves as unlucky said going to the bank when there was a robbery was unlucky. The people who viewed themselves as lucky said getting shot in the arm instead of the head was lucky.

Learning new things is a way of increasing your luck—bringing more connections into your life. Try different educational courses. Travel. Open yourself to new experiences. Read outside your favorite genres. Ask people to teach you about things they're passionate about.

When it comes to writing, one of the best ways to be *luckier* is to write more things. It's common for people to write for years and then one book breaks out. Ten years to become an overnight success. Writing more helps you become a better writer and gives you more opportunities to succeed. I've heard writers talk about how they're worried editors will get sick of them sending story after story to the one market. Assuming you follow the submission guidelines, most editors will be thrilled to accept a story from someone they've sent fifty rejections to. They'll be happy to see your determination rewarded.

While it's important to acknowledge the role luck and privilege play in success, by making more friends, looking for opportunities and writing and submitting more, you can make some of your own luck.

THE STRESS OF SUCCESS

No one tells you how hard it is, having your first book come out. Or, EVERYBODY DOES, but you don't listen, because it's the thing you want most in the world... Suddenly, you're stressing out about a million new things. Sales, reviews, the opinions of random strangers. Hate on Twitter. Love on Instagram. What does this mean for the next one? Will there be a next one? Should I try to do the same thing? Should I do something completely different? It threw me off my writing game more than anything else that's ever happened to me.
  - Sam J. Miller

Here's what they don't tell you about climbing mountains: almost everyone who dies, dies on the way down. The summit as much as you want it, is only the halfway point. And night will be here soon, and there will be no way to go but down, and you will be so tired. I am no climber of mountains, but I am a climber. Will you fall in plain sight, a monument to those who come after you? Will you vanish into the darkest depths, never to be seen again? Take a breath, as well as you can and prepare for the careful climb down. You have a long life still to live and many more mountains to climb.
  - Noelle Stevenson

Beginning writers are sometimes under the impression that once they sell their first book, everything will be smooth sailing. There are plenty of things that can derail writing careers, and sometimes there's disappointment because things don't live up to your expectations. But there are also problems caused by success. Much of this can resolve around the weight of expectation. If your first book is a huge bestseller and wins all the awards then working on your second book can be a terrifying prospect. Everyone's going to be disappointed and know your first book was a fluke. The same thing applies if one of your first short stories wins a major award. People are inviting you to submit to their fancy anthologies and you have no idea how you managed to write the first story and they're going to be so disappointed in the drivel you send them.

Or maybe your dreams have come true, but you're not sure how to handle all the extra attention. Why do interviewers keep asking the same boring questions? Why are you being asked for opinions on topics totally unrelated to your book? You just want to write. You don't want to have to deal with all this business stuff. If you're from a marginalized community, then suddenly you're a spokesperson for an entire cultural group. If you mess up, you're letting everyone else down.

It's rare to get an international book tour and you're so grateful for your publisher's support, but you don't want to spend a month away from your family, and staying in hotels gets tiring really quickly, and you thought there'd be time to see the local sights, but you just want to stay in bed and not talk to anyone ever again, and this was supposed to be your dream life. And if you complain, everyone will think you're spoiled and ungrateful and there are a million hungry writers who would trade places with you in an instant.

There's also the deadlines and the pressure to write sequels. Maybe it took you three years to write your first book and now you're supposed to have two sequels written in two years, and you don't even know what's going to happen in the other books, because you originally thought it was a standalone novel. If you write the same kind of book, you're going to be dismissed as repetitive. If you write something different, you're ruining your personal branding and betraying your true fans.

Social media has made it so much easier for readers to

reach out to writers. It can be wonderful to hear from fans how much your stories have meant to them. But people tag you on social media to let you know they thought your new book wasn't as good. Or they keep asking when the next book is coming out. Or they blame you for things outside of your control like the price of the ebook or why the book isn't available in a particular format in a certain country.

It's good to be hopeful, but it's also useful to anticipate potential issues. Don't assume everything will turn out for the worst, but think about how you'd deal with problems.

Success can also cause problems by giving you more choices and opportunities. More opportunities is usually a good thing, but it can make it harder to keep your focus and choose what to do next. It's good to explore different options—you've always wanted to write a comic book and now you have a chance—great, go for it! Maybe you'll discover that's what you wanted to do all along. But be aware it will take time away from other things you could have been doing. The more options you have, the harder it becomes to determine the worth of each option. If you have three choices, you can research them all, but if you have fifty choices, it's too much work to decide which one to do and you end up doing none of them. Try not to let too much choice make you inactive. If you get stuck, hope-fully there are people who you trust such as your agent or your writing friends who can give you helpful advice.

DIRECTION

WEIGHING THE VALUE OF ADVICE

I have never listened to anyone who criticized my taste in space travel, sideshows or gorillas. When this occurs, I pack up my dinosaurs and leave the room.
  - Ray Bradbury, Zen in the Art of Writing

There's more writing advice available than you could read in a lifetime. Thousands of writers are ready to share their secrets of hitting the bestseller charts. *You must write every day. No one wants to read a book with an unlikable main character. Adding bears to your space opera will increase your sales by 38.4%.* So who should you listen to?

So much depends on context. People giving generic advice don't know your circumstances. What worked for them may not work for you. What worked twenty years ago may not work now. For almost every situation there are conflicting generally accepted pieces of wisdom. *Fortune favors the brave. Fools rush in...* The specific details are often more important than generic wisdom.

The Internet is full of obviously nonsensical statements which you can confidently ignore. *Women don't write science fiction.* Beware of arbitrary milestones or cut-off points. *If you haven't done x by y, you'll never do z.*

Be wary of people drawing conclusions based on statistics from dubious sources. If someone is talking about average author earnings decreasing, are they talking about full-time writers? Full-time novelists? In India? Statistics can be manipulated to fit an argument. Are author earnings falling because publishers aren't paying as much, or does it mean there are more part-time writers included in the survey compared to the previous one?

When I wrote a short story about an intergalactic team

of librarians, I divided the librarians into summarizers and verifiers. Information retrieval won't be as an important issue compared to the ability to summarize and verify information. This was before the *Fake News* scandals of recent years. Verifying the accuracy of the information you're given is an important task. When it comes to studies purporting to tell you the best way to live your life, remember that sample sizes are often small and the results often vary depending on the context. Psychology has been going through a so-called *replication crisis* in recent years, where the results of many influential studies are unable to be reproduced.

Survivorship bias is another thing to consider. People who succeed often have the same goals and try the same things as people who fail. If you ask one writer how they wrote a bestselling book, they might tell you they wrote the book they wanted to read. If you ask writers who didn't make the bestseller list, they'll tell you the same thing.

How much weight do you give to *encouraging* advice versus *realistic* advice? Should you be worried if someone says that most writers never get a book published? It's important to be realistic about your expectations, but you shouldn't give up hope. In *Making Hope,* psychologist Shane J. Lopez says to be wary of phrases like: "*Our kind of people just can't do that. You're not college material. You should be grateful for what you have. You were never really good at that. You have to be rich to make it.* They all reflect a fixed mindset, and reinforce the destructive notion that the world is permanently divided into *haves* and *have-nots.*"

Beware of *tough love* advice based on insecurity. *I wrote four books in a year and if you can't do that, you're not a real writer.*

Beware of listicles that succumb to the temptation to simplify complex issues. Sometimes they can be great examples of distilled information. Other times they can be inaccurate oversimplifications that fail to capture the nuances of the problem.

Established writers might have a breadth of experience, but sometimes their experiences are no longer relevant to your situation. If you want information about breaking into the industry, asking a recent debut novelist might be more helpful than a writer with a long career.

Just because someone is successful, it doesn't necessarily mean they're a good teacher or that they possess insight into how they achieved their success.

People usually give advice based on their own experiences. If you're from a marginalized group, the person dispensing advice might not have had to deal with the problems you face.

Beware of grand pronouncements that generalize about genres or styles of writing. *If you're writing a space opera, you absolutely must have a character who follows the hero's journey*. It's difficult for a few pithy sentences to capture life's vast complexity. Some people are also prejudiced against commercial genres. In academic settings, many writers have had the experience of being told they should forget about writing genre fiction and instead focus on *important* literature.

What about career advice from your publisher or agent? You want to at least consider their advice, but people often have different goals from you. Sometimes they're simply wrong.

Be especially wary of predictions. *Leprechauns are going to be the next vampires! The market for novellas is going to collapse within a year!* People are lousy at making forecasts. When it comes to things like the stock market, expert predictions are often worse than random picks.

What about when you get conflicting feedback on a story? One person in your critique group tells you the ending made them weep and it's the best thing they've ever read. Another person says the ending is awful and a complete betrayal of the story's heart. The common wisdom in this scenario is to listen to the person whose feedback best matches your vision for the story. What if you wrote a rough draft for a workshop and you don't know what the story's about yet and fifteen people are telling you to do totally different things? The more often you get feedback on stories, the more familiar you'll be with working out what kind of advice is useful for you. Sometimes it can help to put the work aside for a while. If everyone is telling you the same thing—the opening is too slow—then it's probably a good idea to listen to this advice.

THE EXPECTATION OF PROGRESS

For the first couple years you make stuff, it's just not that good. It's trying to be good, it has potential, but it's not. But your taste, the thing that got you into the game, is still killer. And your taste is why your work disappoints you. A lot of people never get past this phase, they quit. Most people I know who do interesting, creative work went through years of this… And if you are just starting out or you are still in this phase, you gotta know its normal and the most important thing you can do is do a lot of work.

 - Ira Glass

Be patient toward all that is unsolved in your heart and to try to love the questions themselves like locked rooms and like books that are written in a very foreign tongue. Do not now seek the answers, which cannot be given you because you would not be able to live them. And the point is, to live everything. Live the questions now. Perhaps you will then gradually, without noticing it, live along some distant day into the answer.

 - Rainer Maria Rilke

You never really succeed. You always fail at a higher level. As a screenwriter, the first level of failure is you can't finish your screenplay. I saw a lot of those people in film school. Then you finish the screenplay, and nobody wants to read it. Then you get somebody to read it, and they're not interested. You get them to read it and they're interested, but you can't sell it. Then you sell it, but it's not made into a movie. Or it's made into a terrible movie that you're embarrassed to be associated with. Or, you know, you hit the jackpot. You get the movie made, it's a critical success, it's a box office success—and everybody turns to you and says, Okay, you gotta do it again.

When you're confronted with a difficult task, the expectation is that it will get easier with time. Writing is not always like that. Maybe you start writing and have a couple of breakout short stories and then can't sell anything. It's common to have a dry patch after you make your first professional sale. It's not that it was a fluke, it's just that each story is different. Sometimes the more you learn, the more different things you try and they don't immediately work. I made my first professional short fiction sale when I was eighteen. More than twenty-five years later, I still haven't managed to sell a novel.

You know that writing isn't easy. You don't expect to sell every story. You know your first few stories might not be any good, but you're prepared to work hard. You're going to clock up those 10,000 hours to achieve mastery. You've gone to writing workshops and you know you're a better writer. A few years have gone by, but you still can't sell anything. What's going on?

There's no one easy path that everyone follows. Some people have early success and then struggle, others gradually improve and reach a point where they sell most of what they write. Other writers can break into a couple of short story magazines, but no other markets are interested in what they write. Don't look for scientific formulas for how this is all supposed to work.

Famous writers are often asked for the shortcut to writing success. *Read more. Write more. Don't give up. Write what you love. Find friends who support you.* There really aren't any other universal secrets.

It can be dispiriting when your rewards don't match the amount of work you put in. You spend years working on your craft, then that annoyingly talented new writer wins all the awards with their first ever story. Or maybe you spend years writing a novel and no one wants to read it, and you spend a couple of hours dashing out a short story and it wins all the awards. But the next things you write all suck, and maybe it was a fluke after all, and none of this makes any sense.

In language learning, people talk about the *intermediate plateau*. It's easy to get stuck at a level where you know enough of the language to get by in a basic conversation, but it's hard to push yourself to achieve fluency. It's tempting to view writing the same way, but the problem is that each book and story is different. Successful writers are always learning new things.

Another thing is that your expectations shift, so it feels as though your end goal got further away. You dreamed of getting a story published, and then you meet other writers who are doing all these amazing things and you realize there is so much more that you want to do.

Writers who have sold a couple of things but are still mostly getting rejections sometimes want to know what they have to do to *level up*. There were writers who toiled for years and then suddenly started selling everything. What changed? Sometimes it's just to write more things. They are getting more rejections than before, but they are also selling more things. Other writers only see their sales and assume they are now selling everything. Some writers say that once they started aiming for more emotional impact (rather than trying to write clever ideas or twists), they started selling more. Other writers say that adding more subtext worked for them, that once they tried to have the same text working on multiple levels, their stories became richer. This isn't a book about craft. There are many other books that can help with that. It might be worth getting an experienced writer (especially one known for giving insightful feedback) to critique some of your work and give you feedback about your writing in general.

Try not to be discouraged when it feels like you're not making progress or you're going backwards. It happens to most writers. Keep going.

CHOOSING WHAT TO WRITE NEXT

The best writing advice I have to give is to write whatever the hell your strange, beautiful heart desires.
  - Alyssa Wong

It's rare to see much advice on how to choose what to write next. One of the reasons is that it's such a personal decision. The standard advice is to write whatever excites you the most. But what if you have ten ideas and you're super-excited about all of them and you can't even get started on one, because that would mean giving up immediately starting work on the other nine projects. So you spin around, unable to start anything. Or maybe you write a chapter and stop because you know the next shiny thing is going to be soooo much better and you never end up finishing anything. Or maybe you've done all the work and researched the market and you've written five novels and nobody was interested in them and now you can't muster any enthusiasm about any of your projects.

Sometimes it comes down to a choice between two things and you want to ask agents and publishers which one the market would be more interested in. Lots of people will tell you that you should ignore the market and write whatever you're passionate about. But what if you write a book in your favorite genre and then when you look at agent submission guidelines, so many of them say don't send us *whatever genre hit really big two years ago*? Maybe someone will still publish it if it's good enough and distinctive enough, but why would you make things more difficult? The problem with following market trends is that you'll often be behind—it can be too late by the time you hear about the trend and finish a book. Trends change all the time and can differ depending on category. *No one is buying boy wizard stories. Unless it's an interactive picture book boy wizard story set in Australia. We can't get enough of those!*

If you have an agent, ask them which of your ideas they'd be most enthusiastic about trying to sell. Try some pitches on writing friends and see which ones they get most excited about.

If your books sell well, you might be pressured to write sequels or books set in the same universe. You need to work out if that's what you want to do. If you want to write something completely different but are worried about confusing your existing readers, you could consider a pen name. Some writers such as Neil Gaiman are lucky enough to have devoted fans who will read anything they write and hop across genres. Iain Banks wrote general fiction under that name and wrote science fiction under Iain M. Banks.

If you're a novelist and want to experiment with different styles, you could try writing some short stories.

One of the most exciting and challenging things about writing is there are so many different ways to make things. It's important not to treat yourself too harshly if you feel overwhelmed and unable to choose. This quote from Marissa Lingen sums up a lot of the angst and joy associated with creative choice. "You are not failing if you can't do literally everything at once... Choice paralysis is not just for grocery shopping. It's a real thing in creative fields. So I see other people do this, and I do this: we do choose. We stop running in circles and choose. And then we beat ourselves up for not being the quantum superposition of all to-do lists. It's a good thing if you have a lot of exciting ideas. It is a good thing. It does not mean that you are broken for not doing all of them yesterday."

MAKING WORDS

MY NOVEL WRITING PROCESS, AKA WRITING WITH BABY

Aliette de Bodard

Aliette de Bodard lives and works in Paris. She has won three Nebula Awards, a Locus Award and four British Science Fiction Association Awards. Her space opera books include The Tea Master and the Detective, a murder mystery set on a space station in a Vietnamese Galactic empire, inspired by the characters of Sherlock Holmes and Dr. Watson. Recent works include the Dominion of the Fallen series, set in a turn-of-the-century Paris devastated by a magical war, which comprises The House of Shattered Wings, The House of Binding Thorns, and forthcoming The House of Sundering Flames.

This essay was originally published on Aliette de Bodard's blog.

There's a fabulous essay by Ursula K. Le Guin on writing and motherhood, which contains the following: "The point, or part of it, is that babies eat manuscripts. They really do. The poem not written because the baby cried, the novel put aside because of a pregnancy, and so on. Babies eat books. But they spit out wads of them that can be taped back together; and they are only babies for a couple of years, while writers live for decades; and it is terrible, but not very terrible."

I read this years ago, and it's stuck with me (though I'd forgotten that awesome last part). It's all so true; and even more so when you have the actual baby. I stopped writing about seven months into my pregnancy, because I spent most of my time lying down with no energy, feeling very much like a beached whale. After the birth of the snakelet I struggled with not writing, so I started doing it again in fits and starts; but it wasn't until the snakelet was 4-5 months old, and I was almost ready to go back to work, that I started writing my novel again.

Novels, for me, are different commitments than short stories: I can research a short story for weeks and binge-write the actual first draft in a couple of days; I just can't do that with a novel. With novels, I have to sit down and write consistently; a little at a time for a long time. The problem, when you have a baby, is that "little" can mean three minutes before something goes wrong ™ and you have to rescue a crying snakelet from whatever he got himself into.

I've seen people post about setting some time in the week for writing, always the same time: it never worked for me pre-baby, and it certainly didn't work afterwards (when something does need your attention, it's a choice of me or my husband; if my husband isn't available it has to be me. In those circumstances, a set schedule is a bit like mission impossible). My philosophy was: "whenever there is available time, grab it". Didn't matter if it was ten minutes while the baby napped or while my husband played with him; I just used whatever I had.

"Available time", though, doesn't get you very far with a day job and a baby. When I started up the novel again, I was 25k in, and needed to get to 100k in a couple of months: simple maths told me I would need to write more than 1000 words a day to make my self-imposed deadline. Given that there were a lot of days when I just couldn't manage to write, this sounded like a lost cause.

Fortunately for me, I have a commute. And an alphas-mart (a Neo 2 I think). They don't make them anymore (they stopped around 2013), but those things are the best friend for a writer like me. Basically, it's a keyboard with a small screen. I admit the attraction, put like that, is limited, as you could get the same mileage out of an iPad or a laptop. But the thing is, a Neo is totally distraction-free, boots up in a heartbeat, (you touch a button, it lights up, you touch a button, it turns off), and it keeps going *forever* (and I mean forever. I got mine in 2009, I put three AA batteries in it, and it's still at 60% despite my typing up 1.5 novels, 1 novella and a bunch of short stories on it). You only get a chunk of 10,000 words or so (after that you need to change memory buffers, which is trickier), but given that you can't really edit with it, it's fine for me. I basically would type my day's scenes on the Neo, transfer it to my laptop (it hooks up to computers by pretending to be a keyboard, which means it's dead easy to set up), and do cleaning up and editing on my laptop.

The trouble with this method is that I need a lot more editing afterwards, because I make a lot more typos and because scenes easily get very repetitive (the Neo screen has about 6-8 lines of text on it? not ideal to get a large-scale picture). I did a lot of things in Word, and then imported the lot into Scrivener, where I searched for repetitions and moved stuff around (Scrivener is a very powerful tool that's good for a lot of things; my use of it is akin to using a kitchen robot to chop up a few cloves of garlic: that is to say I label different scenes according to their POV, and move scenes around in my draft).

I didn't *quite* make my deadline (of course), but I was still pretty darn close. Certainly, if you'd told me I'd write most of my novel while minding a very young child a year ago, I would have had my doubts.

NO WORD IS EVER WASTED

Delilah S. Dawson

Delilah S. Dawson is the award-winning author of the New York Times-bestselling STAR WARS: PHASMA. Her books include the Blud series, the Hit series, SERVANTS OF THE STORM, and the Shadow series, written as Lila Bowen. With Kevin Hearne she co-writes the Tales of Pell. Her creator owned comics include Sparrowhawk and Ladycastle, and she's written comics in the worlds of Marvel Action Spider-Man, The X-Files, Adventure Time, Labyrinth, Rick and Morty, and Star Wars Adventures and Forces of Destiny. www.whimsydark.com.

This essay was originally published on Twitter.

So here is a secret: Not everything I write goes anywhere. I have at least four books completely written and edited that never went on submission. I have books that stalled out at 20k. I have one-page documents on my computer with opening paragraphs I don't remember writing. But!

Every now and then an idea sticks with me like that corner of tortilla chip that just won't go down your throat. It happened with *Sparrowhawk*, which began as 40k of a YA book, died, and was reborn as a comic. It happened with *The Willows*, a short story that began as an attempt to sell a Romance but turned out to be a Southern Gothic horror story.

Even the bones of *The Willows* screamed strangeness, not sexiness. I loved the taste of the world, but I hadn't found the right story yet. I tried to write it two more times and failed. I let it lie dormant for years. Until I finally understood what it was.

I took the fifty pages I'd written and cut half of them,

twisting the story around from a dark romance inspired by the band *The Civil Wars* and turned it into a spooky descent into madness. And it looked back at me from the abyss as if to say, DUH.

Sometimes a bit of story comes to the writer like a child playing Telephone. Just a whisper, and you might mishear it. But it bothers you, sticks with you. It's okay if that little snippet takes years to grow and take root. You won't lose it; it will pull at your sleeve, refusing to be lost. Because what you have is a puzzle piece. Ideas often arrive to us piecemeal, and the pieces will fall into place as your subconscious and your working mind finally land in step with the right story. This isn't writer's block or your muse dancing away—it's just part of the process.

I used to write down all my ideas, but then I realized that in eight years, I'd never gone back to my journal to mine it for snippets. The stories that are strong enough to grow nestle in my mind like seeds. I couldn't forget them if I tried. One day, I know they'll make sense.

Don't fall into the mindset of believing one sort of story has more merit than another. At first, I felt bad that *The Willows* wasn't going to be a full-on book, like I wasn't doing it justice. But a short story, novella, or comic is a valid form of art. Some stories need visuals. Some stories hinge on the gut-stab of a twist and will do better with 3000 words than 100,000. Some books fare better as novellas. Some standalones should always stand alone. We need all these forms.

So if a story isn't taking to the page like you'd hoped, it might be worthwhile to consider if the problem is:

- It's more idea than plot.
- Your characters or world aren't fully built

- You're writing the wrong form for that particular story. Is it a journey or a stabbing?

And just because you've written or sold a story one way doesn't mean it can't evolve. Short stories can kick off book worlds. Novels can yield short stories. One scene can spin-off into a comic. It's fluid. No word is ever wasted.

There's a vulnerability to a story that transformed from its genesis. You may second guess yourself. Did I do the right thing? Did I shortchange it? Is it doing what it was meant to do? But that story might be vital to someone. Its odd nature might make it extraordinary.

I'm a big believer in taking risks with your stories. Writing should be play, not work, in that you write for joy and flow rather than external praise. The strongest stories are written because they grab you by the throat, not because you're writing to trend.

If you have an idea that lights you up, don't let it get precious. Don't feel that it has to be some 400k magnum opus, that it must be serious to be meaningful. Just write the heck out of it, in whatever way makes you feel like you're alive and dancing. Take the risk. Fly.

But! A caveat: You won't learn much unless you finish something and show it to the world. My #1 writing advice = 1 crappy finished first draft is worth 1000 shiny new ideas or perfect beginnings. So, yes, play. But finish your work. That's how you learn - through completeness.

Recipe for a 1st draft:

- Identify beginning, inciting incident, conflict, climax, end.
- Craft a protagonist uniquely challenged by the world & conflict.

- Write straight through, front to back, no editing/self-judging.
- If you stall, insert [tk] (to come) and write the next scene you know.

Recipe for a short story:

- Identify the gut punch/twist.
- Craft a protagonist who will succumb to it.
- Create a short, action-filled plot (without infodump/rambling) that will lead to the twist
- Make sure it's self-contained and complete.
- Polish to perfection.
- NO RAMBLING.

Rambling is my pet peeve in short stories. "Kenneth had always enjoyed turtles. The way they floated and breathed through their butts. As a child, he'd…"

NO.

Action and dialogue. Kenneth saves a turtle in the road, and as he returns it to the pond, he meets THE TURTLE KING.

If you're thinking, "But Delilah, you write for *Star Wars* and other intellectual properties. How is that play?" the answer is that it's like being locked in a room. There's still plenty to do in that room. Often, constraints can inspire even greater creativity.

One of the best things I ever did for my writing: Joined a local writing group where we were given timed exercises at each meeting. No planning ahead. On the spot, you had to take the prompt and craft an appropriately-sized story, then read it out loud for criticism.

Point being, you'll better know whether an idea would

work best as a short story, a novella, a novel, a series, or a comic when you've written and edited many projects. You'll probably stall out a few times as you find your feet. Failure is part of the process.

And by *failure*, I don't mean THIS IS CATASTROPHIC AND YOU SHOULD NEVER WRITE AGAIN, because that's not possible. I mean you might try to write a 3k short and it ends up 8k. Or you want a 60k book and it's only 40k. Practice will help you find a project's scope earlier.

Some ideas work best as short stories, novellas, novels, or comics, and the only way you can find out what you're writing is by finishing. Finish everything. Figure out what to do with it later. You'll learn. As long as you're having fun, you're arting right.

SLOW AND STEADY WINS THE RACE

Kate Dylan

Kate Dylan grew up in a sleepy English town where there was little to do but read, watch movies, and bake. After graduating university, she turned her love for storytelling and the visual arts into a full time job, embarking on a career as a video editor. But it wasn't long before she realised that telling other people's stories wasn't quite enough; she wanted to tell her own. Her passion for writing YA novels is (unofficially) sponsored by Smarties and Nespresso, and supported by her long-suffering boyfriend and their two cats.

This essay was originally published on Twitter.

People often ask me how I manage to write novels while working full time, and my answer is always the same: small, achievable goals.

So here's a little secret about me: my daily word goal is 200 words. For some, that might seem like a tiny, why-even-bother number, but 200 words a day has translated to three full novels over the last six years, plus two half novels (one abandoned, and one in progress), as well as countless rounds of edits, revisions, pitches, concept chapters, synopses, bios etc. etc.

Small. Goals. Work.

Why? Because they're achievable on my *very worst day*.

So those days when my boss is an ass, or I was out late, or I'm sick, or just tired of life, those 200 words still get done.

Most days, I write more; I'd say it's closer to 300-400 during the week, 500 on weekends. Often, just forcing myself through those first 200 inspires me to keep going. But when it doesn't—when I have to fight and claw for every word—I can still make my goal. I still feel accomplished. And more importantly, I don't feel like a failure.

As a writer, your brain is going to spend all its time conspiring to make you feel inferior; don't give it another way to do that by setting yourself up to fail. Work out what's *realistic* for you and make that your goal. That's how you form a *sustainable* habit.

Aiming for the moon is great and all, but absolutely pointless if you burn up in the atmosphere before you ever get there.

Here's another tip for forming a habit: accountability. When I first started writing, tracking my word count in a spreadsheet worked wonders for my productivity because I loved typing in the numbers and seeing the total grow.

But these days, it's my writing group that keeps me accountable. We meet once a month so my goal is to have at least *one* new chapter to share at each meeting. Often, I'll manage two. (Sometimes I accidentally vomit 16k words on them in one go—but let's not talk about that.)

The really important thing to remember is that your goal is whatever *you* need it to be. It doesn't matter how many words Stephen King writes, or JK writes, or that dick, Bob, in your writing class who can write a book in a week.

Eyes on your own paper. Find your natural rhythm and don't let anyone shame you for it.

I am a slow writer.

I have always been slow, and I will probably always be slow.

But I get the work done, and that's all that matters.

WHENEVER I'M IN AN EXTENDED PERIOD OF NOT WRITING I AM ALWAYS DEEPLY, DEEPLY MYSTIFIED ABOUT HOW THE HELL TO START AGAIN

Isabel Yap

Isabel Yap writes fiction and poetry, works in the tech industry, and drinks tea. Born and raised in Manila, she has also lived in California and London. She is currently completing her MBA at Harvard Business School. In 2013 she attended the Clarion Writers Workshop, and since 2016 has served as Secretary for the Clarion Foundation. Her work has appeared in venues including Tor.com, Uncanny Magazine, Lightspeed, Strange Horizons, and Year's Best Weird Fiction. She is @visyap on Twitter and her website is https://isabelyap.com.

This essay was originally published on Twitter.

Notes to a future self who will need it, written from a self who has just gotten out of that hole.

Give Yourself Time

You know this part pretty well. The thing is, it's not just plonking down and beating yourself up mentally until the words squirt out. It's actually being generous with that time. And believing you deserve it.

This was a huge problem for me in 2017. I would tell myself *write for two hours on Saturday*, but because I hadn't written in SO LONG, two hours was not enough. I couldn't lower it any further—nor could I be happy with the few sentences I managed in that time.

Sometimes two hours is not enough. Sometimes you do

need to give yourself the expanse of entire day, or an entire afternoon. Sometimes, honestly, you can't afford that time —you have Something Else Important going on. (For me: grad school applications and day job.)

I spent a lot of energy fighting that reality and blaming myself for it. In a way, it *was* a choice I was making, but the truth is: I couldn't do all three things well. I didn't have the time to write. It hurt a lot.

But I knew I didn't want to stop writing. I knew that grad school applications were temporary. So I told myself that when applications ended, I would give myself the time to write—enough time. And real, *free* time—not time over-burdened with guilt.

I didn't know if it would work. But once I got through the application cycle, I told myself to make writing a prior-ity. I would give my brain an ample amount of time to work on the words. And I had planned things carefully so that financially this would be possible for me.

I was HUGELY afraid that I would have giant blocks of time to write and that I would just…not write. I was afraid I would sit down and nothing would come out, just like nothing came out every time I tried to give myself two hours the previous year.

But when I gave myself time—actual time, free time, time to play, time where I was conscious that writing would be my priority—it worked. I've been writing nearly every day for two weeks now. It feels pretty miraculous.

Lower the Bar

You can go lower than that. Lower. You can go even lower. Think of it like this: what's the worst that could happen? You write a shitty sentence? Okay, well. You can fix that sentence in edits. You can kill that sentence entirely. Keep going.

Okay. So *now* you're worried about finishing something and it not being good enough to sell? Well...so what? So you don't sell it. So you try and try and it doesn't go anywhere. That's fine if you like the story. If reading it still makes you smirk, then it's worth *something*.

What's the worst that could happen? The worst is that you stop writing; that you waste this chance past-you set up so you could write. Not writing, in this scenario, is your bad outcome. Bad writing, unpublishable writing, is preferable.

Because right now? The goal isn't publishing. The goal isn't beautiful writing. The goal is that you REMEMBER HOW TO WRITE. You are so, so, so afraid of putting down words on the page, but you can't even remember why. YOU KNOW HOW TO DO THIS. You do. So do it.

Until you remember how to write, that you *can* write; until you recall the bone deep satisfaction of getting words down: you have no other goal. The story can be fail/ridiculous/THE WORST. Get some words down. That's your priority right now.

Feed Your Brain

As much as you love watching dance practice videos and memes on YouTube, or reading hot-take articles and passively browsing stuff on Amazon—some of what you feed your brain with HAS to be story. Really.

Preferably prose. Read those books you've been putting off. Have ten tabs open and gobble up great essays or stories. Sit on a park bench and read. You have to read again. You have to be stuffing your eyeballs with stories. Personally, the best thing for me is reading fiction or fanfiction, but you can substitute these with whatever helps you write best.

Not into the new stuff? Fine. Reread your favorite

fanfic for the tenth time. Read some poetry. Whatever you need to, to start ingesting stories. Then you can expand to filling your brain with other things. Movies, anime, videogames. Stuff with narratives.

Once your brain is back in narrative-mode, you can start going pure visual. Go to museums and write stuff down. Walk in the park and contemplate trees. Get out for a bit. Fill your brain with random visual cues. They'll spark things in unexpected ways.

Get Backup. Have Conversations

Talk to some friends about the story you're working on. Tell them about all the stupid things in it that make you yell and hate things (but that also secretly make you go nyahaha, I'm writing again, it's silly but oh my god I'm *writing*).

They're your friends. The prose doesn't need to be there. Bleat about all the ways this story is ridiculous. Send snippets from your work-in-progress. Tell them where you are stuck because writing flirting scenes is the devil.

You don't have to go it alone. You don't have to nobly wander in the desert wondering how to get your character across a table to deliver a meaningful embrace (does she circumvent the table? Stumble over it? Dodge it?). You can ask Twitter. You can send a friend a crying emoji. It's fine. Lean on your community.

As good as you are at motivating yourself, and finishing stories entirely on your own, it's fun and it does help to have someone else excited about it. Especially since you're so unsure. To have that reinforcement, especially for a work-in-progress, is huge.

Amuse Yourself

Remember why you got into this in the first place? It wasn't about publishing. It wasn't even really about community, although that has since become a huge part of it. And it certainly wasn't about awards.

No, you started writing because you had a story to tell, and you knew that you were the best person to tell that specific story in the way you'd want it to be told. You wanted to write that sentence and get away with it.

You wanted to write about a demon standing pale against the snow; sexy kappas; the urban legend of Ursula from your high school; magical girls who go to a strip club and bleed; Mebuyen and her thousand boobs; bishonen in space...

You've got all these silly ideas that you want to *read* in story forms. You like reading your stories. They amuse you, the sentences seem true to you, and of course—*of course* if they find awesome readers, that's an amazing reward. But you're a reader too.

If nothing else, you should be amused by your story. Like "Haha, I'm actually writing this! Whee!" That's where it started when you were doing mashup multiverse fanfic, age five. It's why you've written all this time. No need to be self-conscious. If it's for you, it's fine.

Other meanings have since gotten tacked onto it, of course. You care about representation, getting things right, pleasing your audience, etc etc. At this point in your career you do want to sell things. I'm not saying that stuff doesn't matter.

But right now, while you're trying to remember how to write, that stuff cannot be prioritized in any way. Instead: wrangle out the story in a way that will get it done, and make sure it's fun for you in the process. That's the core you're looking for, ultimately.

· · ·

Practical Stuff

- Timers are your friend.
- Word goals aren't necessarily your enemy.
- Go to a cafe, dude, you're very productive in cafes.
- Something is better than nothing.
- You're always going to be distracted, it's fine. Just get to work.
- STOP CHECKING TWITTER. Get the words done first.
- If you're serious about it the words *will* come out
- Can't push this story along? Open up your scraps document and just get some words down, you'll feel better
- Copy some A+ prose by hand.

All right, self. This was past you giving you the kick in the ass and the tough love you needed. You'll get it back, dear. You really will. Be patient, clear-eyed, and determined. The words have never left you. They're there. Just start: you'll find them.

I WAS GOING TO WRITE AN ESSAY ABOUT PROCRASTINATION

In his book *The Now Habit*, Neil A. Fiore describes procrastination as "a habit you develop to cope with anxiety about starting or completing a task. It is your attempted solution to cope with tasks that are boring or overwhelming... Procrastination is not the cause of our problems with accomplishing tasks; it is an attempt to resolve a variety of underlying issues, including low self-esteem, perfectionism, fear of failure and of success, indecisiveness, an imbalance between work and play, ineffective goal-setting, and negative concepts about work and yourself."

This doesn't mean you have a fear of failure for every task you've never completed. There are things you put off starting because they're tedious and aren't that important. No one can do everything. But what about projects you really want to do, but never make much progress on? Getting started can be half the battle. Sometimes this is because you're feeling vulnerable about failing. Sometimes it's because you're low on mental energy or are too distracted.

Fiore says "The fear of judgment is the key fear that stems from over-identifying who you are, your worth as a person, with your work. From this fear follows the counterproductive drive toward perfectionism, severe self-criticism, and the fear that you must deprive yourself of leisure time in order to satisfy some unseen judge... In my work with thousands of procrastinators I have discovered that there is one main reason why we procrastinate: it rewards us with temporary relief from stress... Procrastination reduces tension by taking us away from something we view as painful or threatening."

Sometimes procrastination is rewarded. If you wait

long enough someone else might end up doing the work. If you're feeling anxious about applying to a writing workshop, if you wait long enough the deadline will pass and you won't have to write that difficult application essay. In an essay, *Procrastination Is Not Laziness* David Cain writes that "Particularly prone to serious procrastination problems are children who grew up with unusually high expectations placed on them... A procrastinator becomes disproportionately motivated by the pain of failure. So when you consider taking anything on, the promise of praise or benefit from doing something right are overshadowed by the (disproportionately greater) threat of getting something wrong. Growing up under such high expectations, people learn to associate imperfection or criticism with outright failure, and failure with personal inadequacy."

Cain goes on to say that even though he makes lots of plans, he finds ways to work around them. "Planning is something I do very well. I have planned the next day (or week) thousands of times. I've taped it to my door or bathroom mirror. I've set alarms, made promises, left trails of instructional sticky notes all through my apartment. But I am not sure if I've ever executed one of these plans all the way through... It's hard to pinpoint exactly why I'll do anything but what I planned, but it's not that they're necessarily difficult tasks. Sometimes they're so easy that I don't feel any urge to do them right away, and therefore can justifiably do something even easier, like check my email, watch online documentaries, or try a new recipe. My adversary is the unconscious reactive part of my mind, and by now it's a world-class expert at manipulating me. It's like being a prison guard for Hannibal Lecter. Sure he's locked up, but he's Hannibal Lecter."

So how do you avoid procrastination?

Fiore recommends a number of techniques, including redefining how you think about tasks. "Replace *I have to*,

with *I choose to*. Replace *I must finish* with *When can I start*. Replace *This project is so big and important* with *I can take one small step*. Replace *I must be perfect* with *I can be perfectly human*. Replace *I don't have time to play* with *I must take time to play*...
One of the reasons we procrastinate is out of fear that once we start working there'll be no time for play, that work will deprive us of play and the enjoyment of life. Guilt-free play offers you a way around this problem by insisting that you plan recreation in your weekly schedule. Making play a priority in your life is part of learning to overcome procrastination... Attempting to skimp on holidays, rest, and exercise leads to suppression of the spirit and motivation as life begins to look like all spinach and no dessert. To sustain high levels of motivation and lessen the urge to procrastinate in the face of life's demands for high-level performance, we need guilt-free play to provide us with periods of physical and mental renewal."

Play can be writing as well. Something that's just for you and you don't feel obligated to share with anyone. Play could be computer games, TV, or going to a museum with friends. Fiore writes that "British psychoanalyst and pediatrician D. W. Winnicott wrote in his book *Playing and Reality* that it is in playing that we build confidence in the reliability of our creativity and our excitement about discovery —the movement from not-knowing to knowing, from lack of control over problems to control and resolution of problems."

Fiore has a system he calls the *Unschedule*. You create a weekly schedule by assigning time for your leisure activities, work and family commitments and chores. Then you schedule thirty minute blocks for the project you want to work on. "This method of scheduling encourages you to start earlier on your project, because you now realize how little time is actually available for work after you deduct daily chores, meetings, commuting, meals, sleep and leisure. In addition, starting is easier because thirty minutes of work is too little to be intimidating, while it is enough to make a good start and to receive a break or reward... The Unschedule builds your confidence in two ways: first, it gives you immediate and frequent rewards following short periods of work, rather than delaying a sense of accomplishment until the task is completed; second, the habit of recording each period of work gives you a visible reward that allows you to see how much concentrated, uninterrupted work you have completed each day and each week."

Another thing that can reduce the pressure of potential failure is to not only think of yourself as a writer, but to have other hobbies and interests. It sounds counterintuitive, but spending time on other projects can give you more motivation to start writing. Fiore mentions studies that found "the more complex and varied your sense of self, the less likely you are to become depressed over stress in one area, because 'you have these uncontaminated areas of your life that can act as buffers.'"

In her blog post *How Writing an 'Emotional To-Do List' Helped Me Push Past Procrastination,* Kara Cutruzzula talks about recording your emotional reaction to each task on your to-do list. Maybe it's stress or boredom or anxiety. Once you've identified the emotion, take steps to reduce that emotion. If you have a stressful task, schedule something relaxing after it. If you have a boring task, schedule a fun reward for finishing it.

I find that going to writers' conventions is a good way to replenish my motivation. Hearing other writers talking about their cool projects makes me want to start something of my own.

Getting Started

Researcher Tim Pychyl says the act of starting can significantly ease a task's burden. "Once we begin a task, no matter how dreaded, our perceptions of the task change... we don't appraise the task as quite so stressful or difficult once we get started. Starting is everything."

The idea of efficiency is one of the ways I'm able to talk myself out of starting. If I want to learn a new computer programming language, it would be more efficient to wait for the new version to be released. In *Atomic Habits*, James Clear writes about the distraction of optimal plans. "It is easy to get bogged down trying to find the optimal plan for change: the fastest way to lose weight, the best program to build muscle, the perfect idea for a side hustle. We are so focused on figuring out the best approach that we never get around to taking action."

It's tempting to delay starting a novel by focusing on background reading and worldbuilding instead. These are important, but can be seductively easier than writing itself. Some writers prefer to do detailed outlines before beginning a new book. The balance between outlining and working out things as you go is something every writer needs to work out for themselves. And there's no reason it can't vary by project. Outlining can save you a lot of work by helping you focus on what you want to write, but try not to let preparation be an excuse for starting your actual story.

So how do you get started? David Allen's system *Getting Things Done* emphasizes the importance of concentrating on the next action. A large project can feel less overwhelming when you focus on the next step.

When James Clear wants to start a new habit, he designs it so it will take less than two minutes to accomplish. If you want to read more, your habit becomes reading one page before bed. The trick is to make it as easy as possible to get started. Set yourself the goal of writing for two minutes every day. Gradually the habit will become easier and you can increase the time you spend on it.

Creating an implementation plan can help. Instead of *I will write more*, *I will write for thirty minutes every Wednesday morning from 6:30*. Shane J Lopez mentions a study looking at people who wanted to exercise more. One group was asked to develop a *when and where* plan for their exercise. "When participants were contacted months later, 91 percent of when/where planners were still exercising regularly, compared to only 39 percent of nonplanners."

Deadlines

Tim Urban has a popular blog post and TED talk about being a master procrastinator. *The Rational Decision Maker* in his brain is distracted by *The Instant Gratification Monkey*, who doesn't want to do any difficult work. The only way to banish the monkey is by summoning *The Panic Monster*, who appears when a deadline's imminent. It's common for people not to start tasks until the deadline is close. One technique to avoid having to rush at the last minute is to set yourself earlier *fake* deadlines. Ask your editor to give you a deadline a month earlier than the real deadline. Tell a friend you'll have the first draft ready for them to read by a certain date. Make it a realistic target and ask them to check on your progress. If you're writing short stories but can't get started, choose an upcoming anthology which has a deadline and write a story for that. One of the benefits of joining a critique group is they can give you a deadline to submit something for workshopping.

Public accountability can also work for some people. Make a post on social media that you will have your first draft finished by a certain date and ask people to check on you. This can backfire and make you feel miserable if you don't make the deadline, so choose a date you have a realistic chance of making. Another more extreme method is to choose an organization you despise and tell your friends you will donate $100 (or an amount of money you can afford to lose but will still be painful) to the organization if you haven't finished your first draft by the deadline. This can be an incredibly strong motivation—you don't want to be someone who donates to that kind of organization. This method certainly isn't for everyone and you probably don't want to try it when you're writing your first book (because it will almost certainly take longer than you expect). Make sure you choose a realistic deadline and amount of money. It can be a valuable exercise to record how long it takes you to write a novel so that (even allowing for the fact each novel is different) you can get a better estimate of how long the next one will take you.

Finishing

Sometimes getting started is the easy part. You're excited about an idea and have written some fun opening chapters. But time passes and your progress is slow and you get bored. You've got a dozen ideas that are more interesting. So you put your project on hold and start working on the new thing. Then the same thing happens again. How do you avoid the allure of the shiny?

Delilah S. Dawson says that boredom can sometimes mean you should change something about your project. "So when you're writing and your brain says OMG LET'S DO SHINY NEW PROJECT, maybe your brain is really telling you to shake up the current project. To find a scene you're really excited about when you've settled into a predictable pattern of linking scenes. Up the ante."

Sometimes you don't want to expend energy on a

project because you feel it isn't good enough. It's normal to be full of doubt in the middle of a project. Writers are often terrible judges of their own work. There are many writers who felt their novel wasn't worth finishing, but they persevered and the book went on to win awards. N.K. Jemisin became the first person to win three Hugo Awards for Best Novel in a row and says of the first book in the trilogy: "I had a despair moment again while writing *The Fifth Season*. Convinced myself that it was just too strange, too dark, too hard to write, and no one would ever want to read it. I actually called my editor and discussed whether I could just turn the trilogy into a standalone, wash my hands of the whole thing, and go cry in a corner somewhere."

In an interview, legendary director Akira Kurosawa talked about pushing on when you are in the middle of a writing project. "When you go mountain climbing the first thing you're told is not to look at the peak but to keep your eyes on the ground as you climb. You just keep climbing patiently one step at a time. If you keep looking at the top you'll get frustrated. I think writing is similar. You need to get used to the task of writing."

If you're working on a non-fiction project, there will always be more to learn. While it's important to research your topic, at some point you're going to have to finish. I struggled with that with this book. There are so many books on motivation, productivity, confidence, and happiness, and I wanted to read them all. Eventually I had to admit to myself that if I wanted to finish the book, I had to stop reading and start writing.

There's value in completing something and in most cases it's worth the effort to keep going. Problems in a first draft can be fixed in revision. Beware of getting caught in the whirlpool of endless revisions though. At some point you need to accept the book is ready to be read by someone else. You'll probably need to revise it again based on feedback from your critique group or agents or editors. It's worth spending the time to revise the book, but again, you need to declare it finished at some point.

Starting the Next Thing

Make sure you celebrate finishing something—especially if it's a major project like a book. Give yourself a break and do other things you've been meaning to catch up on. But don't let the break go too long. How long is too long varies for everyone. Make sure you have enough time to recharge. I'm good at finishing projects, but it takes me a while to start the next one. Part of that is because I have trouble choosing what to do next and I let myself get out of my writing habit.

THIS IMPORTANT NOTIFICATION WILL REVEAL THE SECRET OF ELIMINATING DISTRACTIONS

But, Lord! to see how much of my old folly and childishnesse hangs upon me still that I cannot forbear carrying my watch in my hand in the coach all this afternoon, and seeing what o'clock it is one hundred times; and am apt to think with myself, how could I be so long without one; though I remember since, I had one, and found it a trouble, and resolved to carry one no more about me while I lived.
  - Samuel Pepys on buying a pocket watch in 1665

Some interruptions can't be prevented. This is especially true if you have young children. But if you're having problems focusing on your writing and find yourself distracted when you sit down at your computer, there are ways to reduce the number of distractions. The Pomodoro technique is the most useful method I've found. Set a timer and write for twenty-five minutes. Then take a five-minute break. Repeat. The fact you're on a timer and know you're not supposed to do anything else but write can help you concentrate. The technique relies on being able to carve out twenty-five minute blocks of time. That's not always possible. I can't use the Pomodoro technique at my day job as a computer programmer because co-workers are always asking questions and I need to respond to critical server alerts. But at home, the technique is one of the best things I've done to be able to write more.

Social media is a big source of distraction for many people. In his book *Digital Minimalism*, Cal Newport writes "It's not that any one app or website was particularly bad when considered in isolation. As many people clarified, the issue was the overall impact of having so many different shiny baubles pulling so insistently at their attention and manipulating their mood. Their problem with this frenzied activity is less about its details than the fact that it's increasingly beyond their control. Few want to spend so much time online, but these tools have a way of cultivating behavioral addictions. The urge to check Twitter or refresh Reddit becomes a nervous twitch that shatters uninterrupted time into shards too small to support the presence necessary for an intentional life."

It's easy to underestimate the time you spend on social media. You can install programs on your computer and phone to track how you're spending your time. (Some people may be worried about the privacy implications of this, so make sure you choose a program with a good reputation). *RescueTime* is a popular program that provides detailed reports on how you've been spending time on your computer and phone.

Some people recommend deleting social media accounts. If social media is making you miserable, that might be the right decision. For most people, social media provides the most convenient way to keep in contact with friends. I've heard the argument that if you delete your accounts you will still keep in touch with the people important to you and the others didn't really matter anyway. But that's not how it works for most people. Especially if you have friends in other countries. And while social media is not necessary for writers, it can help boost your visibility. If you want to run a Kickstarter, it's going to be a lot harder if you're not active on social media.

Keep your social media accounts if they give you value, but reduce your usage if they consume too much time. Set yourself rules. *No social media before breakfast. No social media after ten o'clock.* Pretend you're behind on watching the latest episodes of your favorite TV show and need to stay off the Internet to avoid spoilers.

Turn off notifications on your phone while you're writing. There are ways to mute notifications except from one or two people (for example your partner) that you need to check in case it's an emergency.

Turn off autoplay on *Netflix* and *Youtube*. Make the deliberate decision to watch things rather than getting stuck watching the next thing that's recommended.

Cal Newport recommends going through a digital declutter. Uninstall all the apps on your phone. Try a period of no social media (excluding things you absolutely have to use, e.g. you use Twitter for your day job). He suggests going for thirty days without social media. This might be too extreme for many people, but you want a long enough period that you break out of your habit of always checking your phone. This will let you work out which social media platforms are actually useful for you, and which are time wasters. Reinstall the apps that actually have value for you.

When I moved apartments, I went four weeks without any Internet access at home (this was pre-smartphone) and I was surprised by how much time I suddenly felt I had. Traveling is another way to trial restricting your social media usage. In recent years, I've spent up to three weeks in locations which didn't have any Internet access. That might not be practical for many people, but it does help you work out how useful social media is for you.

Distractions are usually based around convenience. If you make things more difficult to use, you reduce their appeal. If the first thing you do when you wake up is check your phone, then leave your phone in another room. If you find yourself getting distracted while you're on the computer, log out of your social media accounts. If you need something more drastic, use a program like *Freedom*, which restricts your Internet at certain times. Turn off your router and put it in another room.

If you have multiple devices, allow yourself only to use

social media on one of them. Your computer is for work, your tablet is for social media.

Another way to reduce distractions on your computer is to create a separate user account just for writing. Set up a different wallpaper and don't install anything except your writing program. When you log in using that account, you know it's writing time.

Changing your location is another way to remove distractions. Write in a cafe or library. I'm lucky that after work I can walk to the State Library of Victoria which has a glorious reading room with a domed roof. These days most places have WiFi, but don't ask for the password if you want to concentrate on writing. Another option is a co-working space. These might be too noisy, but if you're regularly working from home they can provide the chance for some social interaction.

I've also heard some authors mention using a traffic light system at home. Hanging a green sign on your door means your family are welcome to come and talk. Orange means you're working, but interruptions are ok. Red means don't disturb unless it's an emergency. It might not be practical to implement for everyone, but it can give your family a better idea of when you'd prefer not to be interrupted.

THE GOOD, THE BAD, AND THE OFFLINE

Whenever someone says something shitty about me on Twitter, I find the best medicine is to spend 5 minutes reading their feed. Nothing cures that sting like learning that it's not you, it's them.
  - *C. Robert Cargill*

Being playfully rude to someone who doesn't know you is the exact same thing as being actually rude.
  - *Olive Rae Brinker*

There is nothing cooler than telling people how much you don't like a thing other people like. Don't care about Star Wars? You are a hero. Don't care about the Avengers? Let me shake your hand. Don't care about Game of Thrones coming back? Holy shit where can we put your statue?!
  - *Rob Hart*

Share your enthusiasm, not your rules.
  - *Lauren Panepinto*

How do you balance the joy of connecting with friends and learning about the world, with the vitriol, the hatred directed at marginalized groups, the endless fights, the mansplainers, the mental and emotional impact of a torrent of negative news, the feeling that all your friends are living better lives than you, and the massive amount of time that social media can suck away?

The extreme position is to delete your social media

accounts. If that's what makes you happiest, go for it. You can keep in touch with friends via email and text messages and revel in all your extra free time. Plenty of bestselling authors get by without using social media.

Most people want to keep using some social media because it lets them know what their friends are doing and provides news about the writing and publishing industry. Much of it depends on how you use social media and how you curate your friend lists. Advocates of reducing your social media usage argue that you can keep in touch with your close friends by other means, but this is more difficult when your friends are scattered all over the world.

In *Big Potential*, Shawn Achor writes, "We live in a society where technology allows us to be more interconnected than at any time in human history, and yet, as our mediums for connection have multiplied, our happiness has decreased. That's because we now have an unlimited, continually replenishing supply of negativity available instantly at our fingertips: everywhere from the news apps on our phones to the Twitter feeds and Facebook pages we scroll constantly to the email in our inboxes—and many of us are addicted to it... Our study revealed that individuals who watched just three minutes of negative news in the morning were 27 percent more likely to report their day as unhappy six to eight hours later—it was like taking a poison pill each morning that made all of your efforts, energies, and interactions throughout the day more toxic... Yes, it's important to know what's going on in the world, but our exposure to disproportionately more negative news has an unintended consequence: less faith in our own ability to tackle not just the challenges in the world, but our own lives as well."

If this is the case for you, try implementing rules such as no social media in the morning, or no social media just before bed. Or no social media on the weekend.

My own Twitter feed usually makes me happier—I follow a lot of people who post animal videos. Celebrities such as Kumamon make me laugh. I'm lucky that many of my friends are out exploring the world and doing interesting things and I enjoy learning from them. I'm also aware my view of social media is shaped by the fact I'm a straight white guy and I don't have to deal with microaggressions and online harassment. Social media is a friendlier place for me than for many other people. Anita Sarkeesian's *Feminist Frequency* has an online resource: *A Guide to Protecting Yourself From Online Harassment* with advice on how to deal with harassment.

If you have friends or family who you don't want to unfollow or unfriend, but their posts upset you, mute or hide their posts.

In an earlier chapter, I mentioned Cal Newport's idea of doing a *digital declutter*—a period of no social media usage for a month. Delete all the apps from your phone. After the declutter, work out which programs are useful for you. A month might be a bit extreme for some people, but you want to try for an amount of time in which you can break your regular habit of always checking your phone.

Turn off social media notifications on your phone. It's rare that you need to respond urgently. Don't feel obligated to have an opinion on every latest scandal.

When I'm tempted to write an angry reply to someone, I'll write the reply offline and wait until the next day before deciding whether I want to post a reply. In almost all cases I end up deciding it's not worth it. I have better things to do than argue with people I don't know. Again, this is shaped by my experience as a straight white guy—I'm unlikely to have my personal identity targeted by hateful comments. It's different if you're from a marginalized community and it's also important to speak up to support your friends who have been targeted. (While taking into account how your friends want to you to help—sometimes you can make things worse by engaging a troll).

Social media can be a wonderful thing, but decide the best way it works for you and take breaks when necessary.

ALL THE THINGS YOU KNOW YOU SHOULD DO, BUT DON'T

Habits are the compound interest of self-improvement. The same way that money multiplies through compound interest, the effects of your habits multiply as you repeat them. They seem to make little difference on any given day and yet the impact they deliver over the months and years can be enormous. It is only when looking back two, five, or perhaps ten years later that the value of good habits and the cost of bad ones becomes strikingly apparent... We often dismiss small changes because they don't seem to matter very much in the moment. If you save a little money now, you're still not a millionaire... We make a few changes, but the results never seem to come quickly and so we slide back into our previous routines.
- James Clear

- Sleep more.
- Eat healthier.
- Exercise more.
- Write more.
- Read more.
- Spend more time with your friends.
- Be kinder to others.
- Build your invincible army of the dead.

We all know we should do these things. So why don't we? A lot of it comes down to habit and convenience. We get stuck in routines and do what's easiest. You want to write, but find yourself playing computer games instead.

Sometimes we're pushed to change by circumstances. I was diagnosed with sleep apnea a few years ago. My cpap machine records how many hours I sleep each night. After my diagnosis I read more about the importance of sleep. I hadn't realized how big a difference it can make if you regularly don't get enough sleep. Matthew Walker's book, *Why We Sleep*, is a thorough overview of the latest sleep science. "Routinely sleeping less than six or seven hours a night demolishes your immune system, more than doubling your risk of cancer. Insufficient sleep is a key lifestyle factor determining whether or not you will develop Alzheimer's disease... Sleep disruption further contributes to all major psychiatric conditions, including depression, anxiety, and suicidality... Adults forty-five years or older who sleep fewer than six hours a night are 200 percent more likely to have a heart attack or stroke during their lifetime, as compared with those sleeping seven to eight hours a night." After having my sleep monitored in a sleep lab and reading Walker's book, I increased the amount of sleep I regularly get.

Charles Duhigg's *The Power of Habit* and James Clear's *Atomic Habits* are books I found particularly useful when it comes to changing habits. *The Power of Habit* looks at more of the social aspects behind habits, whereas *Atomic Habits* contains more practical information on how to change your habits. Clear stresses the importance of setting up systems rather than making goals. Goals are the direction you want to go in, but they have the problem of encouraging you not to be happy until you reach that milestone. "I've slipped into this trap so many times I've lost count. For years, happiness was always something for my future self to enjoy. I promised myself that once I gained twenty pounds of muscle or after my business was featured in *The New York Times*, then I could finally relax."

Clear says that you should focus on making your process better. If you can enjoy the act of writing itself rather than the rewards of publication, it can be easier to keep going when you keep getting rejection letters. Finishing a story makes me happy. Of course, I'm disappointed if it gets rejected, but I don't view writing the story itself as a waste of time.

Convenience is a big driver of habits. People do what's easiest. They also respond to cues around them. If you want to increase your chances of maintaining a habit, add visual reminders. Post-it notes on the fridge door. A motivational image as your computer wallpaper. A list of your enemies on the wall.

Clear gives the example of setting things up so you read more—when you make your bed, put a book on your pillow so it's waiting when you go to bed. The opposite is true for habits you want to reduce. If there's a plate of cookies sitting on your bench it's harder not to eat them than if they're hidden in a cupboard. If you make bad habits a bit more difficult to do, it's surprising how much easier it makes to avoid them. "When scientists analyze people who appear to have tremendous self-control, it turns out those individuals aren't all that different from those who are struggling. Instead 'disciplined' people are better at structuring their lives in a way that does not require heroic willpower and self-control. In other words, they spend less time in tempting situations."

In theory, removing a social media app from your phone shouldn't stop you from constantly checking social media. You can reinstall the app any time you want. But making a bad habit less convenient can make it easier to abandon.

Shawn Achor talks about his *twenty second rule*. He makes bad habits twenty seconds longer to do. If he's watching too much TV, he puts the remote control in a different room. He makes good habits twenty seconds easier to start. Have your gym clothes ready to go when you get home.

Setting an implementation strategy makes it easier to start a habit. Decide where and when you'll do the action.

If you make the plan to write for thirty minutes every morning at 6:30 at your desk, you're more likely to start than if your plan is to start writing some day.

H*abit stacking* is when you find something you already regularly do and add your new habit to it. Clear gives the example of pairing the habit of changing out of your work clothes with the habit of changing into your gym clothes. Make it a routine action, something you don't need to think about. You don't need to expend willpower making the decision, it's just what you do. *After I put the breakfast plates in the sink, I'll write for thirty minutes.*

Although it's not a practical solution in most cases, changing jobs or moving cities gives you opportunities to break out of bad habits. Remember that the next time you change jobs or move. If you're getting distracted by things at home, try writing at a cafe or library instead. The first time I went on a long overseas vacation by myself let me see how many things I'd been doing out of habit, such as watching television every night. After I returned to Australia, I reduced the amount of television I watch.

Everyone has different workloads. I live by myself and I don't bring home work from my day job. At the end of the year I often make grand plans for what I want to accomplish next year. I'm going to finish a couple of books, I'm going to write all the short stories. I'm going to learn a new language. I'm going to write a computer game. It's easy to take on too much. That's one of the reasons New Year's resolutions so often fail. Small changes are more likely to be successful than grandiose plans. Start as small as possible. Clear aims for a new habit to only take two minutes when he's starting. Write for two minutes in the morning. Once you've developed the habit, expand the time you spend on it.

In an online essay, Gregory Ciotti recommends setting macro goals and micro quotas. "Your goals should be the big picture items that you wish to someday accomplish, but your quotas, are the minimum amounts of work that you must get done every single day to make the bigger goal a reality. Quotas make each day approachable, and your goals become achievable because of this."

While it's generally a good idea to start small, sometimes a drastic change is the best way to get something done. Quitting my job and traveling around the world for six months was one of the best ways I improved my life. It depends on you and your circumstances.

Think about how you can fit new habits into your schedule. If you're going to be on the train for thirty minutes every morning, look at ways you can use that time. Instead of walking to the station closest to my apartment (which is five minutes away), I walk to the next station, which gives me twenty minutes of exercise every morning.

Use your phone or computer to remind you to do habits. I have a script on my computer that starts playing a song from the *Sorry to Bother You* soundtrack at 6:30 every morning. When I hear the song I know it's time to write.

Prepare *If Then* mental models in advance for events likely to challenge your habit. If someone offers you a cigarette at the party, you'll say no. Clear also talks about developing your identity in terms of your habit. Someone who says, *No thanks, I'm trying to quit* versus *No thanks, I don't smoke.*

The *Don't Break the Chain* method (popularized by Jerry Seinfeld) is a way of sticking to a daily habit. Each day you complete a set period of writing, mark it on a calendar (forming a chain). You have a visual reminder to encourage you to not miss a day. If you look on places like Etsy, you can find people selling fancy calendars you can use to track your progress. You can even order *The Bubble Wrap Calendar*, which has a bubble to pop for each day you complete your chosen task.

There are plenty of habit tracking apps that allow you to do the same thing. There are even apps which let you set up a financial penalty if you don't complete your habits.

It's also possible to gamify your habit tracking system. *Habitica* is an online habit tracking system that lets you create a character and level them up when you maintain your habit for a certain amount of time. You can even go questing with other users. If you all complete your goals, you can defeat monsters and gain more experience points. I found it a bit too much work to set things up, but some people love the gaming aspect of this.

Measuring your progress can be an important way to help maintain a habit. Some people get really enthusiastic about measuring data about themselves. The Quantified Self movement is a community based around "self knowledge through numbers." Stephen Wolfram (the founder of Wolfram Alpha) has kept a record of every keystroke he's typed since 2002—all 100 million of them!

I'm not quite as focused as that, but I've been tracking the number of books I've read each year since 1991.

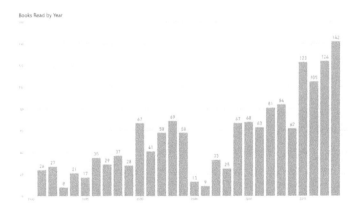

Books Read by Year

There's a big dip when I moved to Japan in 2005. Moving to another country and starting a new job meant I didn't have as much time for reading. Plus in pre-Kindle days it was harder to get English books in Japan. There's a big jump in 2015 when at the start of the year I made a shortlist of the books I wanted to read that year.

Once you start measuring something, there's always the temptation to artificially increase your score. If I read shorter books, I'll be able to raise my score. Make sure your desire to increase your score doesn't interfere with what you really want to be doing. You also want a method of tracking your progress that doesn't require much work. You don't want to make your habit more difficult.

Many writers record the number of words they write each day. Ultimately getting the words written is the important thing. The downside is it's harder to track editing—if you spend the day revising and your word count ends up negative, it might not feel like a productive day. I prefer to keep track of the number of Pomodoros (twenty-five minute focused sessions) I do each day. Use whatever system works best for you.

You can use a spreadsheet to track your word count. If you're a fan of chart art you could use a charting program (or Excel) to make some pretty graphs. If you prefer something physical, draw a table in a bullet journal, or use stickers to mark your progress. My system is to drop a glass gem (a board game component) in a bowl each time I finish a Pomodoro session. I like the sound the gem makes when it drops in the bowl and the physicality of it. At the end of the month I end up with a bowl full of gems showing how much work I've done.

At some point all of your meticulously planned schedules will fail. A life event will intervene. A death in the family, a new child, a new job. You'll miss your daily writing habit and you'll miss it again. You'll think that since you've already broken the chain, it's okay to miss a few more days. Everyone needs a break. The problem is that starting a second time is often more difficult. In the back of your mind is the reminder that you *failed* the first time, so what's the point in trying again? That's one of the reasons New Year's resolutions are popular—they give you permission to restart what you tried before. If this is a problem for you, one way to counteract this is to give yourself permission to pause your habit, rather than stopping it. Many apps give you the option to skip rather than break the chain. You haven't failed. You're just putting things on hold while you deal with a personal crisis. When that's finished, you'll resume your habit (rather than start over).

IF ONLY I COULD FIND THE PERFECT TO-DO LIST APP, I COULD CONQUER THE GALAXY

One thing at a time. Most important thing first. Start now.
- Adam Westbrook

Top Three Tips for Writing Productively
1. Set goals!
2. Incentivize productivity! (e.g.: allowing yourself that devilish slice of cake for finishing your word count!)
3. Walk into the woods until you find a black well in a dead clearing. The thing inside will name a price. Pay it.
- Sam Sykes

Many people are familiar with the idea of setting *SMART Goals*—Specific, Measurable, Attainable (or Achievable or Assignable), Realistic (or Relevant), Time-based.

I want to write more becomes *I'm going to work on my novel for an hour every morning.*

It can also be important to distinguish things you have control over from those outside your direct control. *I'm going to work on my novel* versus *A major publisher is going to buy my book.*

There are lots of different productivity and organizational systems, it's a case of finding which one works for you. Which way of setting weekly goals works for you?

A) Set 5 goals. Finish 5 goals.
B) Set 3 goals. Finish 4 goals.
C) Set 10 goals. Finish 6 goals.

Objectively, C is the best because you got the most

done (assuming people aren't waiting on things you told them would be finished). But a lot of people find A or B more satisfying. You might feel as though you've let yourself down with C. Maybe the following week you won't get anything done because you stop taking your estimates seriously. Jeff VanderMeer's *Booklife* is a useful guide for more advice on how to set writing goals.

There's an abundance of to-do list apps that let you track tasks and reminders. Experiment with a few and work out which works best for you. It depends on which operating systems you use, how often you have access to a computer versus a phone and whether you want to share task or event lists with family members. One of the issues is that there are now so many to-do list apps that it would be easy to spend more time testing them than the're going to save you. Since I'm a computer programmer and do project planning, I can legitimately spend time at work testing different project tracking tools. Part of my weakness is that I get excited about using a new tool, try it out for a couple of months, get bored with it and then try the new shiny tool. Since I'm a computer programmer, there's also the temptation to build my own program, one that works exactly the way I want it to. I have to remind myself that this is a trap, one which would take far more time than any such tool could possibly save me.

Workflowy has been one of the most useful programs for me—an outlining tool that makes it easy to quickly add and edit lots of tasks. I use *Workflowy* for my daily to-do lists and *Google Calendar* to remind me of events. I track monthly and yearly projects and goals in *Trello*.

Kanban boards are popular in IT. A kanban board divides tasks into *To Do*, *In-Progress*, *Done* (or similar) columns. Each task gets its own card and gives you a quick visual indicator of how things are progressing. It can be especially useful if you're working in a team because it lets you easily see other people's progress. *Trello* is one of the most popular programs which let you create a kanban board, but there are plenty of others. You can also use a physical board or sticky notes on the wall to show your progress.

Try to find a system you enjoy. Digital systems have the advantage of being accessible in more locations, but some people find the physical act of crossing out an item on a piece of paper more satisfying.

Charles Duhigg's *Smarter Faster Better* talks about how the satisfaction of completing a task can encourage people to prioritize easy tasks over important ones. He recommends setting a stretch goal as well as SMART goals. This is an ambitious goal that doesn't necessarily fit the SMART criteria—it doesn't even have to be realistic. The idea is that aiming high will help you achieve more. When you combine this with smart goals, you're still achieving things, but you also have a lofty goal to aim for. One of my stretch goals was to visit 100 countries. When I was 42 years old, I visited my 100th country, Iran.

Recording which long-term goals you've reached can remind you of your progress. First story published. First translation. First novel. You could add a list to your *Awesomeness Dossier*. Or you could have a bullet journal with your goals in it. Christie Yant created a writer's bingo chart —a spreadsheet you can use to record your completed goals. I wanted to learn how to do some image processing for my computer programming work, so I made a goals tracker that reads in a text file and generates an image with a star chart and planets representing completed goals. That's maybe a bit excessive for most people, but I enjoyed making it.

The Pomodoro technique is the most useful method I've found for increasing my productivity. Set a timer for twenty-five minutes and focus on a task. Then take a five-minute break. Repeat. Before I started using it, I would have an afternoon set aside for writing and I'd write for an hour, then I'd end up watching videos or reading social media for a couple of hours. The Pomodoro method helps me focus more easily and it's how I track my productivity. I completed *x* Pomodoros today.

Forest is an app and web site based around the idea of working on one task for a set period of time. Once the time is over, the app rewards you with a tree in your digital forest. If you interrupt your task by checking social media, your tree withers away and dies. It's a fun program that gives you a visual reminder of your work. The version I tried didn't give an auditory notification when the time period was over though, which meant it wasn't as useful for me. It does make me want to create my own program where you get to build a medieval city. Ah well. I'm going to file that idea in my *one day* project folder.

Shared accountability can be a good motivator. Share your weekly or monthly to-do list with a friend. Have a check-in session at your writing group. If you're writing a novel, find a novel accountability buddy. Check in to see how they're doing and swap critiques when you have drafts ready. For the past five years I've shared monthly to-do lists on a *Trello* board with writing friends. Knowing that other people are watching your progress can be a powerful motivator.

I also join in *word wars* with other writers in a *Slack* chat program. Set a time limit, e.g. thirty minutes, start writing and then check in after the time's up to compare how many words you wrote.

When I was doing research for this book, I heard about a web site called *FocusMate*. You log in and make appointments with other people for fifty-minute co-working video chat sessions. When the session starts, you briefly introduce yourselves and tell each other what your goals are for the session. Then you get to work. At the end of the session you check in to see how you both went. The idea of video chatting with strangers might not be for everyone (and it might shatter your dreams of spending the day writing in your pajamas), but I've found it really helpful. It's less tempting to get distracted if you know someone's watching. The first time I logged in I chatted briefly with a PhD student in São Paulo who was working on her thesis. Then I had a session with a writer in Amsterdam, followed by one with a teacher in Berlin. Since then I've started using the site regularly.

David Allen's *Getting Things Done* is a popular organizational method based around recognizing that unsorted tasks consume your mental energy. When you get a new task, work out whether it's actionable or not. If it's not actionable, file it in your reference folder. If it's actionable and it will take under two minutes, do it straight away. It's not worth the effort of organizing it. If it's going to require more effort, file it so you can retrieve it at the appropriate time. When you have time to work on tasks, choose them based on context or priority or energy available. The system isn't tied to any particular implementation—you could use manila folders or software to track tasks. Allen also recommends doing a weekly review to see how your system is going and how you're maintaining your projects. This is only a brief introduction and there are plenty of overview articles online, as well as Allen's book. I use some of the Getting Things Done ideas, but not the whole framework (which feels like too much effort to me).

If you prefer the physicality of pen and paper, the Bullet Journal method is a way of combining a journal, a diary, and a to-do list. You add page numbers, an index, a future log (to remind yourself of events and tasks in future months), a monthly log (what's scheduled for this month) to your journal and then write daily logs showing your tasks and notes. Writing on paper is one of the simplest and fastest methods of getting thoughts down quickly. At the end of the month you go over your outstanding tasks and if they're still worth doing, migrate them to the next month's log. Your journal can be as simple as you like, but some people take the opportunity to decorate their journals, transforming them into gorgeous works of art. There are online tutorials that give the basics of the bullet journal method.

When making plans it's important to keep most of them realistic (your stretch goal might be the one ambitious exception). People are bad at estimating how long projects will take. IT projects are notorious for taking longer than expected. Part of this is because they're dealing with unknown situations, and it's also due to deciding exactly what the software is supposed to do and how businesses are supposed to change. Another factor when estimating schedules is that when someone asks you how long a task will take, you often think of the best case scenario. How long will it take to update the web page? Ten minutes. Maybe it will take ten minutes to update the code, but I might need to get a manager to check the page in a test environment first to make sure it's what they wanted. Then they realize there's another change, and then the sys admin decides it's a good time to reboot all the servers and I can't test the changes and on and on. If you're a freelance writer, being able to accurately predict how long it will take to get tasks done is an important skill, especially if you're quoting costs in advance.

How good are you at estimating how long it will take to write a novel? You've set yourself the task of finishing your novel by the end of the year. Is that a realistic goal? The answer of course is, it depends. The first time you write a novel it's hard to judge how long it will take. After you've written a few novels, you'll be able to make better estimates. Of course, novels vary widely in size and complexity. Every writer works at a different speed. Try not to get disappointed if you're a slower writer. It takes me a long time to plan a novel and I always underestimate how far I've got to go. Remember to allow for things to go wrong, and the time you'll spend waiting for other people to get back to you. Then double your estimate of how long it will take.

Tasks tend to fill the time they're allocated. If someone gives you a year to write the book, it's unlikely it will take you less than a year. If they'd given you two years to write the same book, for many people it would then take two years. One way to get around this is to set your own deadlines. Even if you have a year to get the book done, if you know you're going to be busy with other things when the book is due, set yourself a six month deadline instead.

Another thing to consider is that it's good to allow some flexibility in your schedule. If you're *super efficient* and have filled all your time, you won't have any time when a better opportunity comes along.

When it comes to the actual process of making more words, experiment with different ways of writing to find what works best for you. Typing versus writing on paper versus dictating. Writing in the morning versus the evening. Writing for long bursts versus short breaks. Rachel Aaron's book *2k to 10k* details her process of increasing her daily word count. She identifies three key areas which helped: knowing what she was going to write before she sat down, experimenting with finding her ideal writing place and time, and writing what she was enthusiastic about. I didn't find much in the book that was helpful for me, but some friends rave about the book.

Another part of productivity for writers is how you keep track of your notes and ideas. This is especially important if you're writing a secondary world fantasy epic series and need to be able to remember how the forty-fifth grand vizier murdered the members of the imperial family and what happened to all of the pieces in the emperor's magical chess set. There are a multitude of ways of keeping notes. Pen and paper are hard to beat for ease of use, but I miss the ability to easily search text and back up my work. There have been attempts to create smart notebooks—the *Rocketbook Everlast* is designed to make it easy to take a photo of a page and it will automatically upload to your cloud provider of choice. But they still require that extra amount of work that discourages me from using them.

Notekeeping software changes all the time. *Evernote* was popular for a while, but I found it too slow and cumbersome. Then they changed their terms of service and it fell out of favor. Many writers use *Scrivener* to keep track of their research (as well as writing their novel). Windows has *OneNote*. I'm fond of keeping notes in plain text files (this won't work if you want to include images!). Text files are easy to work with on every platform. I have a folder with notes for a book and open all of the files in a text editor like *TextPad* or *Notepad++* which allows me to easily switch between files.

If you're more technically inclined there's also the option of creating your own wiki. I like the idea of doing this, but for most of my writing, I know I'd spend more time setting it up than it would save me. If you're writing books set in the same world then creating a wiki might be more valuable. There are programs like *wikidPad* or *VoodooPad* which let you create your own wikis. *Notion* is a new all-in-one workspace program which also includes wiki and database capabilities.

I also keep *common tasks* files. These are not just writing-related, they are tasks I occasionally do, but not often enough that I remember how to do them. I write down the instructions, making it easier the next time I have to do them. This includes things like how to use regular expressions when searching in Word, or how to download backups of my web site, or how to create files for uploading to Amazon.

There are different ways of tracking story submissions or agent queries. You don't want to accidentally send a story to a market which has already rejected it. In most cases, a spreadsheet is the simplest solution. You can also use an online tool like *The Submission Grinder*. I'm reluctant to use online trackers because I want access to my history when I'm offline (I can often go for days without Internet access). I keep my submission history in text files. They're quick to edit and work on every platform. They're not as clean as a spreadsheet and lack features like showing me how many days a story has been out on submission. Since my submission history goes back to 1991, it would be a bit of work to move it into a spreadsheet. I'm tempted to write my own submission tracker database, and have to keep telling myself to avoid the siren song of building everything myself.

It's also worth familiarizing yourself with text expansion tools and shortcuts. These differ by operating system (I use *AutoHotkey* on Windows), but they can save a lot of time. You specify a shortcut and a block of text that will replace it. For example, if I type *-pubs*, it's replaced with a copy of my standard cover letter that I use when submitting short stories.

Experiment with different productivity systems and to-do list methods. Generally, the simpler the method, the better. You don't want something that feels like too much work to maintain. It should be easy to see your next task and easy to update your lists.

NO DEATH MATCH HERE: SELF-PUBLISHING
VERSUS TRADITIONAL

S.L. Huang

S.L. Huang is an Amazon-bestselling author who justifies her MIT degree by using it to write eccentric mathematical superhero fiction. Her debut novel, Zero Sum Game, came out from Tor in 2018, and her short fiction has sold to Analog, Nature, and The Best American Science Fiction & Fantasy 2016. She is also a Hollywood stunt-woman and firearms expert, where she's appeared on shows such as "Battlestar Galactica" and "Raising Hope" and worked with actors such as Sean Patrick Flanery, Jason Momoa, and Danny Glover. She currently lives in Tokyo. Follow her online at www.slhuang.com or on Twitter as @sl_huang.

This essay originally appeared in The Thrill Begins.

I had the unusual experience of having my self-published debut series picked up by a Big Five publisher. My first novel, *Zero Sum Game*, was released by Tor Books in 2018. Having had that experience, I'm not keen on the advice out there saying either method of publishing is categorically better!

I am a huge proponent of having both self-publishing and traditional publishing available as options; I think it's great that people are able to pursue different paths and make different choices for getting their books to readers. What I'm less fond of is the "us vs. them" approach some people take to the question. Publishing paths aren't religions, and sneering at authors who choose one option or the other is bizarre and exhausting. Instead, I think the best way to look at the various choices is as a business and personal decision.

・ ・ ・

Defining Your Goals

Lots of writers go into publishing with different goals. Are you looking to make a career and a living off writing? Do you want prestige or critical acclaim? Maybe you only care about having readers. Or maybe your primary goal is having a product you are proud of. For some, the crowning moment is being able to hold a book they wrote in their hands.

Speed can also be a factor, as self-publishing is much faster than the timeline of New York. For instance, though I'd already decided on self-publishing for other reasons, when I put my first book out, I was in the middle of getting through my second bout with cancer. Impatience not having a place in a writing career is a truism often spouted in publishing, but sometimes there are legitimate reasons to want your book out faster!

Sometimes a goal can point directly toward one path or the other. For example, if you want to have your hands in every part of the process and control it to your absolute satisfaction, that might point more toward self-publishing. Whereas wanting to see your book in bookstores and libraries would lean the calculation toward traditional publishing. For other goals, such as aiming to become a career writer, the answer is less clear, and a lot of other factors are going to play in. But defining those goals can still be a good starting point.

And don't forget that it's also very possible to be a hybrid author. Most reliable studies I've seen even suggest that hybrid authors are out in front of everyone else financially. For writers whose work spans a long career, the answer might very well be different for different books, or even different for the same book at different times.

・ ・ ・

Different Types of Books Do Better in Self-Publishing Versus Traditional

So what types of books do better than others in self-publishing? In my experience and observation, they're usually (1) genre fiction, (2) in a series, (3) novels published fast one after another. Of course there are exceptions, but if an author of literary fiction worked for seven years on a manuscript and came to me asking for advice, I'd be telling them to query agents. It's tempting to think that any novel good enough to get picked out of the slush pile would also take off as an indie title and vice versa, but I don't think that's true at all.

Niche books can also do well in self-publishing—if a book has a small but fervent audience, it might not be enough to attract a publisher, but could gain a solid following online.

On the other hand, the best self-publishers I've seen don't even write the book first. Instead, they're capable of writing to market—studying the lists at online retailers to see what's selling well that's within their authorial wheelhouse, and then writing novels fast to fit that need. This is a skill I don't have myself, but one I admire!

However, it's worth noting that making the choice to self-publish a particular *book* isn't synonymous with going for a self-publishing *career*, even for someone who wants to be a full-time writer. For example, many mostly-traditional authors have added a layer to their income by self-publishing their backlist titles. Others self-publish quirky or off-beat projects, in consultations with their agents, while keeping a mostly-traditional career. Going in the other direction, some self-publishers successfully make deals for print editions or subsidiary rights on their titles, or occasionally take a publisher's offer while still keeping the majority of their titles self-published. There are as many career variations as there are authors who are publishing.

. . .

Different Types of Authors Do Better in Self-Publishing Versus Traditional

But what if you're trying to decide where to aim for the main thrust of your career?

Most saliently, being a self-publisher means being a *publisher*. You have to wear a lot of hats other than the writing one. Not everyone wants to do this, and that's totally legitimate.

I ended up not being as good at self-publishing as I really needed to be to make it a long-term career. By the time I got the offer from Tor, I'd realized a publisher was a much better fit for me. Here are some of the skills great self-publishers have that I lack:

- Writing fast. The best self-publishers can put out a new novel every three to four months. I was only able to release every nine months.
- Market analysis, then writing to market and making sure to do keywords and categorization that would hit those hot subgenres.
- Tracking sales throughout promotional efforts and pricing strategies to nail the best business choices. I did promos, but I found continual and thorough tracking to be exhausting and could never keep it up.
- Gaining expertise in the ins and outs of things like Facebook advertising and Amazon advertising (and having the capital to do so).
- Heavy engagement with readers. I like talking with my readers, but I'm too shy and wary of imposing to try things like street teams.
- Turning on a dime when you see what works and what doesn't.

Not all self-publishers do all of the above, but that's a lot of what I see from the rock star indies. I was successful in putting out a good book that got great reviews, but I struggled hard with the sales-driving parts.

However, probably the biggest reason I fit better with a traditional publisher is an emotional one: wearing all the publishing hats was burning me out. I wasn't even doing it as well as I should have, and I knew trying to add any more on the business/sales side would tax me even further. Now that I'm traditional, the work I do for my publisher isn't *less* work, but it's much better aligned with the way my brain works. It's still hard, sure, but it's not the type of effort that wrings me dry.

On the flip side, some people get a real thrill off being able to experiment with all aspects of the publishing process and being able to control every piece of it. Those people might feel the same emotional burnout trying to balance a publisher's needs as I ended up feeling self-publishing!

Be Suspicious of Anyone Who Tells You There's One True Way

I'm not going to name names, but some people in the industry seem . . . very, very invested in "proving" that one method of publishing is better than another, or looking down at people who make different choices. Some even declare the "numbers" prove it one way or the other—but trust me, I'm a mathematician, and they're wrong. Both indie and traditional have their own drawbacks, but both are also robust, vibrant paths with lots of opportunity.

Choose what seems best for you and your books. There's no one option that's universally best for everyone.

. . .

But What If I Don't Succeed? What's My Option Then?

The more I talk to other writers, the more I come to understand: all writing careers have ups and downs. It seems shockingly unusual for a writing career to soar toward success on an entirely smooth, upward trajectory.

But when you're just getting started, even gaining a foothold can be harder, and it can feel like it takes the "choice" element out of the question of publishing paths. For instance, what if you query a bunch of agents and don't get any bites? What if you self-publish your books and only hear crickets? What then?

In every one of these scenarios, there are still ways forward. Just for example:

- If you know you really want a traditional deal, and you haven't gotten any agent bites? Maybe set the first book aside temporarily, write another book, and then try for representation on that one. It's totally possible for a first book to be published second or third, after a different book launches the author's career, and plenty of authors have followed that path.
- If you know you want to give self-publishing your all, but your first attempt has flopped? *Keep publishing.* Usually, a single release is not enough to give a self-publishing endeavor enough traction anyway. If a few rapid releases don't garner any interest, you can switch series, genres, or pen names and give it another go until you find something that sticks.
- And you can always, always change your mind as you discover what works best for you.

A writing career can be a lot of hard work and repeated stumbles, but there's never a point at which you must declare failure and can never move forward again. And don't let anyone tell you otherwise!

THE LONG ROAD

Illustration by Tom Gauld

THE UPS AND DOWNS OF A LONG CAREER

Martha Wells

Martha Wells is a science fiction and fantasy writer, whose first novel was published in 1993. Her most recent series are The Books of the Raksura, for Night Shade Books, and The Murderbot Diaries, for Tor.com. She has also written short stories, media tie-ins for Star Wars and Stargate Atlantis, YA fantasies, and non-fiction. Her work has won the Hugo, Nebula, Locus, and Alex Awards, and appeared on the New York Times Bestseller List and the USA Today Bestseller List.

So I've been doing this a long time.

My first book (*The Element of Fire*) was sold to Tor Books when I was 26. Because of a contract disagreement, it took almost a year of negotiation before the sale was final. Then it took a year to go through the editorial pipeline and came out in 1993, when I was 28.

Because of that year of contract negotiation, being suspended between the dream of being a pro writer and the reality of having to say no to a bad contract, I never had a rosy idea of what being a pro writer was like. I had first started trying to submit stories to magazines in college, where I worked on the student-run SF/F convention AggieCon, which at that time had an attendance of around 1500 people. I had taken local writing workshops with SF pros, I had worked with them for convention events, I had listened to writing panels and gone to seminars. I knew writing professionally was not easy, I knew the first sale was not an end to rejection, I knew writers didn't suddenly become rich, I knew most of them had to have day jobs. I think that gave me a much more realistic picture and prepared me for the long hard grind that a writing career can be.

Having a debut novel was still very stressful, especially for anyone who had issues with anxiety and depression. Even with everything I knew, for my first four to five years as an author, I felt like I was winging it.

Now for first time authors, things happen very fast. You can monitor your book's progress after its publication practically in real time, and you know very quickly if things are going well or things are going meh or things are going terrible. There's not much you can do about it, but you know, for what that's worth.

The thing that we often don't think about is that good things that happen are just as stressful as bad things that happen, and can cause the same symptoms. You can be overwhelmed by suddenly having a big busy career, mentally exhausted by all the decisions and new deadlines, physically exhausted by the travel, especially if you have a day job and/or a family to take care of or health issues. And you can't talk about being overwhelmed and exhausted, because so many people want to be where you are; it feels ungrateful or like you're bragging. Like you're a rich person complaining that her pile of diamonds is heavy. And this inability to vent makes being tired and overwhelmed worse.

I went from a Nebula Nomination for *The Death of the Necromancer* pretty much straight into a slow motion career crash. (This is when your sales numbers drop low enough that publishers aren't interested in buying any more books from you.) My mother was diagnosed with Alzheimer's while I was writing *Wheel of the Infinite*, and a cocktail of various personal and day job issues made the situation even more stressful. The *Fall of Ile-Rien* trilogy, which was supposed to be my breakout hit, got dumped into the market and sank from sight.

At the time, it didn't really register. In 2006 and 2007, I had short stories, a couple of tie-in novels, fantasy novels and non-fiction articles published. These were the biggest years of my career so far. But by mid 2008, no publishers wanted to buy my books.

A friend described a career crash as: you have been fired from your job but no one tells you that. You keep going to work, and still no one tells you. Eventually you realize that no one wants you there and that they have stopped paying you.

But if you still want to be a professional writer, you have to keep writing. During the crash years, I started a lot of novels that died on the vine in the first few chapters, something that had never happened to me before. I wrote fanfic to save my sanity, and I fired my agent. I wrote *The Cloud Roads*. I queried an agent who had solicited me when *The Death of the Necromancer* came out and was dismissed by an assistant who said they were only interested in books by established authors.

I finally found a new agent who was awesome. But publishers were still not interested in *The Cloud Roads*. While it made the rounds for two years, I wrote *The Serpent Sea*, and *Emily and the Hollow World*. Readers would say how they wished I wrote faster; I was writing faster than I ever had before, but no publishers were buying. I had interactions with other pros who made it clear I was one of those women SF/F writers of the dim past, who was expected to maybe self-publish a little and then fade gracefully away. It was clear to everyone that it was time for me to give up. I started to make plans to find another job. Then boom, *The Cloud Roads* sold to Night Shade Books and I was back in the show, starting all over again.

I finished the *Books of the Raksura* series and started an SF novella, *The Murderbot Diaries: All Systems Red*. Now I'm a

Hugo and Nebula Award winner and a New York Times Bestseller.

Some advice, for what it's worth:

You don't have to be a pro writer to be a writer. A lot of people write as a hobby and never sell their work and get a lot of enjoyment and fulfillment out of it. But if you want to be a pro writer, you have to keep writing. It's a job and you have to keep showing up for it.

Stay current with your field: everyone gets busy and some people only make time to read their friends' new books. Read new writers, read award nominees, keep pushing your comfort zone further and further out until you can't find the edges. Push yourself to continue to grow and evolve with your writing. Don't let yourself get stale.

Find out all you can about publishing. If there's any part of the process you don't understand, read up on it. If something upsets you, make sure you understand the situation first. Remember you can ask your agent, you can ask other authors. Don't ask your non-publishing friend who will sympathize with you and egg you on and who has less than a clue about what's going on.

There's a combination of talent, work ethic, practice, knowledge, persistence, pursuit of experience, and luck that makes a writing career. And to paraphrase Beyoncé and Captain Picard, you can do everything right and still fail; that's just the way life is.

WRITING, MOSTLY

E. Catherine Tobler

E. Catherine Tobler has never had a moment's doubt in her writing career. Never ever ever. Nope. No way, no how. Or has she??? Among others, her short fiction has appeared in Clarkesworld, Lightspeed, Apex Magazine, and on the Theodore Sturgeon Memorial Award ballot. Follow her on Twitter @ECthetwit or her website, www. ecatherine.com.

An earlier version of this essay was originally published on E. Catherine Tobler's blog.

I wish I knew what I was doing.

I've been publishing for eighteen years now (writing for even longer?!), and still don't know. What the hell is this? Writing is the most frustrating job. Are there performance reviews? Promotions? Bonuses? Vacation ti– aahahahaa.

A long time ago, a friend said "I will not walk into the ocean today."

I turned that into a story. (Eventually my friend did walk into the ocean—not all stories end happily.) I will not walk into the ocean today.

The ocean, full of dark and sea monsters, always beckons. I wish I knew what I was doing.

Eighteen years is a long time. It'll probably go on a bit longer, right? Eighteen years—more than 100 short stories. Some novel-shaped stories. Nothing that's done…anything, really.

A story of mine ended up on a ballot once. It's one of the best stories I've ever written, about distance and longing and about having a thing and also not having a thing, and how that's beautiful in its own right.

It's kind of like writing, right? Having a thing, and not.

Existing in a space where you do the work, but few take notice. I can sell short stories like they're hotcakes, but after that... Silence all the way down.

When it's award season, there are Huge Lists about Awesome Writers & Their Fictions One Should Consider For Awards and Glitter Ponies, and I've been reading through the works, because there's a lot that goes right by me—there are So Many Stories, right?

I've written novel after novel, and have queried agent after agent, and have received no after no. *This isn't marketable! I am not in love with this Very Weird Idea! I don't know how to sell this!* But some people, your helpful brain reminds you, don't have to write novels to get agents. They just have them because their short work is brilliant and Does Stuff. Mmm. Well.

Authors who've been writing a lot damn less have collections, Elise, because their work resonates and Says Stuff. You've never ever been in a Years' Best, Best Of, Best Bested Bester, because your fiction just... Well. No one knows. Who even reads it? What does it even do—you aren't exactly on Lists Of Merit. So.

And I wish I knew what I was doing.

Writing, mostly.

There *are* some things I know.

Showing up is only half the deal.

You want to be a published writer? Showing up is huge, but it's only half the battle. Doing the work is the other half. You can sit in all the coffee shops you like, with your cute laptop and your foamy milkycoffeedelicious drinks, but if you're not doing the work, you're not reaching the end.

If you want to be a published writer, you write the scene.

You write the scene that comes after that.

You write the next scene.

Write the next one.

You repeat until you can type THE END.

This is called doing the work.

Worry about what you can control and only that.

Writers tend to worry about things they can't control. *What will people think about my work? What happens if no one reads my work? What if I get a bad review?*

Absolutely none of these are the end of the world. (Oh, it *feels* like it, but it's not.)

Chances are, you will get a bad review.

Chances are, someone will dislike your work.

(Both of those means someone *read* your work. Breathe!)

Will I end up on a ballot? Will I get a shiny rocket?!

Here's what you can control:

- What you write.
- What you finish.
- What you send into the world for publishers to consider.

Have you done the work? Have you typed THE END? You control how you work.

Return to point one. Showing up is only half the deal.

Write.

Truth: real life happens to everyone.

Truth: your years of work will be overlooked.

Truth: no one will value your writing space or time the way you should.

If publishing matters to you, write the scene.

Then, write the next one.

Write the next one.

Write the scenes until you can write THE END.

Writing is not magic—though it can feel that way when it's going well. Writing for publication is like any other job. It consists of hard work. Of putting words down, of stacking up pages, until you have all the pages that story contains.

You have to do the work.

Some stories work.

Some stories don't.

You won't know which you have until you stack those pages and reach THE END.

Write the scene.

Then?

Write the next one.

IF YOU HAVEN'T WRITTEN SEVENTEEN INTERNATIONAL BESTSELLERS BY THE AGE OF FOUR, FORGET ABOUT A CAREER AS A WRITER

It is easy to fall prey to the idea that writing success is intrinsically bound to youth. Publishing loves a literary ingénue, as if no one over the age of 40 or 50 or 60 has anything worthwhile to say... The older I get, the more I have to say and the better I am able to express myself. There is no age limit to finding artistic success. Sometimes it happens at 22 and sometimes it happens at 72 and sometimes it doesn't happen at all. No, you are not too old to have a writing career, no matter your age.

- Roxane Gay

To tell me my old age doesn't exist is to tell me I don't exist. Erase my age, you erase my life—me. Of course that's what a lot of really young people inevitably do. Kids who haven't lived with geezers don't know what they are. So it is that old men come to learn the invisibility women learned twenty or thirty years earlier... In less change-oriented societies than ours, a great part of the culture's useful information, including the rules of behavior, is taught by the elders to the young. One of those rules is, unsurprisingly, a tradition of respect for age. In our increasingly unstable, future-oriented, technology-driven society, the young are often the ones who show the way, who teach their elders what to do.

- Ursula K. Le Guin

From the age of 6 I had a mania for drawing the shapes of things. When I was 50 I had published a universe of designs. But all I have done before the the age of 70 is not worth bothering with. At 75 I'll have learned something of the pattern of nature, of animals, of plants, of trees, birds, fish and insects. When I am 80 you will see real progress. At 90 I shall have cut my way deeply into the mystery of life itself. At 100, I shall be a marvelous artist. At 110, everything I create; a dot, a line, will jump to life as never before. To all of you who are going to live as long as I do, I promise to keep my word. I am writing this in my old age. I used to call myself Hokusai, but today I sign my self 'The Old Man Mad About Drawing'.

- Hokusai Katsushika

Try not to succumb to the idea that if you haven't published a book by a certain age you'll never have a writing career. Regular celebrations of youth (The 30 Hottest Writers Under 30!) make it harder, but older writers have advantages in terms of experience. There are many examples of writers publishing books and stories later in life. Jack Williamson won the 2001 Hugo and Nebula awards for a story he wrote at the age of 93. Sadie and Bessie Delany were 101 and 103 years old when they published their best-selling biography *Having Our Say—The Delany Sisters First 100 Years*. Older artists can still find success in youth-obsessed areas of entertainment. Compay Segundo, a member of *The Buena Vista Social Club* won a Grammy at the age of 90. Olivia Wilde tells the story of asking Tilda Swinton for advice and Swinton told her that with age comes, "self-assuredness and clarity about one's identity... I can just be very specifically me." There's a freedom to being older and not feeling the pressure to conform to other people's expectations.

There are certainly more awards and grants aimed at younger writers, but that doesn't mean people aren't interested in your stories. Sometimes being older means having regrets about things you wish you accomplished when you were younger. *Why didn't I start writing earlier?* You can't change the past. Making peace with what you've done and looking forward to the future is an important part of growing older.

Don't assume younger writers have everything easier though. Don't make disparaging comments about younger generations as a whole! Some older writers have struggled to adjust to social change and have made unpleasant and ignorant comments about marginalized communities. Take the time to at least read introductory articles on things like transgender issues and cultural appropriation.

IF YOUR CAT DOESN'T WRITE 1000 WORDS A DAY, YOU'RE NOT A REAL WRITER

We rarely engage in self-righteous judgment when we feel confident about our decisions: I'm not going to practically knock myself unconscious with a shaming eye roll about your nonorganic milk if I feel good about what I'm feeding my children. But if doubt lurks beneath my choices, that self-righteous critic will spring to life in not-so-subtle parenting moments that happen because my underlying fear of not being the perfect parent is driving my need to confirm that, at the very least, I'm better than you.
- Brené Brown

Some people argue that you need to write every day to be a *real* writer. The uncountable instances of bestselling and critically acclaimed writers who only occasionally wrote disproves this idea. So why do people keep repeating this rubbish advice?

Part of it's because people are insecure about their own status as a writer. As Brené Brown points out, if you're insecure about your own status, you're likely to feel threatened by examples of people doing things differently.

Another part of it is that if you want to develop a habit, doing it every day makes it easier. Some writers stop writing every day and find it hard to start writing again, and therefore conclude that to be a real writer, you must write every day.

It does make it easier if you have a set time of day to write. You don't need to think about it. It's just when you write. In many cases, consistently writing a small amount of words is going to add up to more than doing the occasional burst of writing would achieve.

Writing every day isn't an option or even desirable for

some people though. Iain Banks is one of my all-time favorite writers. He wrote twenty-nine books by writing for only three months every year. Banks said on his writing habits: "I chatted with Terry Pratchett years ago and it seems he has the war of attrition approach. He'd write just a few hundred words per day and keep at it, only occasionally giving himself Christmas Day off. Whereas I'd do nothing for almost eight months of the year, and then write like mad for three months when it's cold!"

Don't listen to anyone who tells you need to write every day.

It should be noted that the one absolute requirement for being a real writer is that you must post photos of your pet online at least once a day.

ENABLING ENERGY SAVER MODE

Sometimes you're motivated to write, you know what you want to write, you've made time to write, but you don't have the mental or physical energy to make words. Sometimes this is because you're exhausted after a long day at the office or looking after children. Sometimes it's due to depression or chronic illness. For many writers energy management is more important than time management. Part of it can be identifying the time when you're most productive and protecting that as writing time. I have more energy in the morning, so I get up earlier to write before my day job.

Sometimes it's general fatigue and taking better care of yourself can help. Schedule time for play. Sometimes you're bored and need a change. A stressful job can leech away your mental energy. If you have a day job where you're required to write, for example as a journalist or a technical writer, it can be difficult to work on your own writing.

Having uncompleted tasks can sap your energy if you're constantly thinking about them. David Allen, the author of *Getting Things Done*, advocates having an appropriate process to deal with incoming tasks. A system for sorting your tasks can make you feel less overwhelmed. Allen recommends sorting tasks into different categories so they're easy to access when you have time to deal with them. I find *Workflowy* a useful web site and app for keeping track of tasks.

Sometimes life events will seem overwhelming. You lose your job, a family member dies, your children have health issues. For some people conserving their energy and taking a break from writing is the best thing to do. Give yourself the time to deal with important life events. For other people, making the time to write can prove to be a useful distraction. Making words can be an area of life that is still under your control.

What if your energy is limited due to chronic illness or depression? Christine Miserandino's influential essay, *The Spoon Theory* talks about what it can feel like to deal with chronic illness. She explains to a friend in a diner that a spoon represents the resources required to perform an action. She only has a limited number of spoons available each day and needs to carefully choose how she will spend them. Many people find spoon theory a useful metaphor for how they cope with their illness. One criticism is that it can give the idea that if you conserve your spoons, you will have more available the next day, which for some illnesses isn't true. Writer Naomi Chainey has criticized the wider adoption of spoon theory, saying it's appropriation when healthy people use spoon theory to describe their "entirely normal fatigue... Spoon Theory was intended for the chronically ill. There's a fair argument that it applies to mental illness and people on the spectrum. It's hardly a universal disability experience though, and the appropria- tion effectively erases the concerns of a marginalized group."

Cynthia Kim blogs about autism and her recommen- dations for conserving energy revolve around identifying which tasks sap most of your energy and whether you have different amounts of energy to deal with social versus phys- ical tasks. "Identifying the cost of activities becomes a crucial conservation strategy... Sometimes, no matter how elaborately I structure, change, accommodate, plan and think about conserving my spoons, I'm forced to admit that something important will still have to go... I don't like to lose and giving up things I like doing because I can't do everything feels like losing. Which is silly, because there is no losing at life."

THE SUPERFLUOUS THINGS THAT WEAR OUR TOGAS THREADBARE

It is the superfluous things for which men sweat... the superfluous things that wear our togas threadbare.
*   - Seneca*

If you can see a thing whole—it seems that it's always beautiful. Planets, lives... But close up, a world's all dirt and rocks. And day to day, life's a hard job, you get tired, you lose the pattern. You need distance, interval. The way to see how beautiful the earth is, is to see it as the moon. The way to see how beautiful life is, is from the vantage point of death.
*   - Ursula K. Le Guin, The Dispossessed*

Sometimes it's the small daily accumulation of problems that wear people out. Someone gives up their dream of being a writer and can't say why they stopped, other than it all got too much. Sometimes it's that people spend so much energy on the pursuit of the superfluous things—accumulating followers on social media, asking people to like their author page, and filling their Twitter feed with nothing but endless promotion. It can be fun to experiment with different strategies, but make sure you leave enough energy for your writing.

Some people are only interested in the glamorous writer life—they want to go on book tours, be interviewed by Oprah, and go to the premiere of the movie based on their book, but they're not interested in sitting down and writing. If you only pay attention to famous writers when they're talking about their career successes, you're missing the close up view. The dirt and rocks. The hard job of putting in all those solitary hours.

Work out what recharges your writing energy. Don't underestimate the value of giving yourself treats. Find what encourages you and gives you the motivation to keep going. Maybe it's decorating a calendar with stickers to represent the time you've spent writing. Maybe it's getting to watch your favorite anime after you've done a day of writing. Maybe it's saving up to visit the city in which your favorite novels are set. What gives you the strength to sit down and make the words?

THE EDGE OF THE MAP

It is good to have an end to journey toward; but it is the journey that matters, in the end.
   - Ursula K. Le Guin

It's funny that pirates were always going around searching for treasure, and they never realized that the real treasure was the fond memories they were creating.
   - Jack Handey

I love maps. As well as the aesthetics of illustrated maps, depicting complexity in a simplified form can allow you to see new things. In my computer programming job, I'm always advocating that people make diagrams of how they think new processes are supposed to work. When it comes to writing, it's clear that *Submissionland* is fraught with peril. *The Whirlpool of Endless Revisions. The City of Social Media Distractions. The Empire of Snarky Reviewers.* Acknowledging these dangers exist helps you mentally prepare for potential problems. It also can serve as a form of consolation that you're not alone in your struggle. There's nothing wrong with you if you're feeling sad about not being able to sell anything for a while after your first sale.

It can help to frame negative events so they're as narrow in scope as possible. *This story got rejected by this magazine this time.* It's not that everything about your writing sucks. The rejection doesn't necessarily mean the story's bad. It's just that the editor doesn't think it's right for them. So much of what people consider a good story is due to personal taste.

One of the keys to enjoying being a writer is finding

the balance that's right for you. The balance between anticipating problems and not being anxious about them. The balance between motivating yourself to keep writing and not being too hard on yourself. The balance between being confident and acknowledging there are things you don't know. Try to find a group of writing friends who will support you. Everyone knows a well-balanced party is the key to a successful quest.

Aim high, but celebrate your small wins. It's important to celebrate your successes, but don't put off being happy until you achieve a certain goal. Remember the joy that comes with seeing your name in print. Try to find happiness in the writing process itself. Sitting down to write doesn't have to be fun or wonderful all the time. Sometimes it's going to be frustrating and painful. But if you can take pleasure and derive a sense of accomplishment from the act of creating a story, this will make it easier to keep being a writer. Finishing a story makes me happy. I'm disappointed if it doesn't get published, but I'm still happy I created something.

It's easy to feel discouraged if you're not on the bestseller lists. Why isn't everyone on Twitter talking about how they're dying to read your next story? You never can tell which of your words are going to have an impact on a reader's life. Even if only a few people read your story in a small magazine, maybe one of them will discover a sentence or idea that resonates with them.

Not all stories have to be *meaningful* with a capital M. Fun and entertainment are important too. A story that makes people laugh makes the world a happier place.

Maps are wonderful and make it easier to get where you want to go, but there's a joy in wandering off the map. Making your own path is sometimes the best way to travel. Roll the dice. Revel in the experience.

FURTHER READING

I don't necessarily agree with everything in these books and articles, but they have some useful information in them. For example, the findings about the effectiveness of power posing in Amy Cuddy's *Presence* have been called into question, but the book still has other useful advice.

BOOKS

THE WRITING LIFE

Bird by Bird; Anne Lamott; Anchor, 1995

Booklife; Jeff VanderMeer; Tachyon, 2009

Word Work: Surviving and Thriving as a Writer; Bruce Holland Rogers; Invisible Cities; 2002

HAPPINESS

When Likes Aren't Enough: A Crash Course in the Science of Happiness; Tim Bono; Grand Central Life & Style; 2018

The Antidote: Happiness for People Who Can't Stand Positive Thinking; Oliver Burkeman; Farrar, Strauss and Giroux; 2012

Man's Search for Meaning; Viktor E. Frankl; 1946

Stumbling on Happiness; Daniel Gilbert; Deckle Edge; 2006

Notes on a Nervous Planet; Matt Haig; Canongate; 2018

Lost Connections: Uncovering the Real Causes of Depression—and the Unexpected Solutions; Johann Hari; Bloomsbury; 2018

Making Hope Happen; Shane J. Lopez; Atria; 2013

The How of Happiness; Sonja Lyubomirsky; Penguin; 2008

21 Days to Resilience; Zelana Montminy; Harper One; 2016

The Happiness Project; Gretchen Rubin; Harper; 2008

Gratitude; Oliver Sacks; Knopf; 2015

Learned Optimism: How to Change Your Mind and Your Life; Martin E.P. Seligman; Free Press; 1998

The Geography of Bliss: One Grump's Search for the Happiest Places in the World; Eric Weiner; Twelve; 2008

CONFIDENCE

Daring Greatly: How the Courage to Be Vulnerable Transforms the Way We Live, Love, Parent, and Lead; Brené Brown; Avery; 2015

Quiet: The Power of Introverts in a World That Can't Stop Talking; Susan Cain; Broadway Books; 2012

The Charisma Myth; Olivia Fox Cabane; Portfolio; 2012

Presence: Bringing Your Boldest Self to Your Biggest Challenges; Amy Cuddy; Little, Brown and Company; 2015

HABITS & MOTIVATION

Getting Things Done: The Art of Stress-Free Productivity; David Allen; Penguin; 2001

Willpower: Rediscovering the Greatest Human Strength; Roy F. Baumeister and John Tierney; Penguin; 2012

Atomic Habits; James Clear; Avery; 2018

The Power of Habit; Charles Duhigg; Random House; 2014

Smarter Faster Better: The Transformative Power of Real Productivity; Charles Duhigg; Random House; 2017

The Now Habit: A Strategic Program for Overcoming Procrastination and Enjoying Guilt-Free Play; Neil Fiore; TarcherPerigee; 2007

Digital Minimalism: Choosing a Focused Life in a Noisy World; Cal Newport; Portfolio; 2019

Better Than Before; Gretchen Rubin; Broadway Books; 2015

Nudge: Improving Decisions About Health, Wealth, and Happiness ; Richard H. Thaler & Cass R Sunstein; Penguin; 2009

SUCCESS

Big Potential: How Transforming the Pursuit of Success Raises Our Achievement, Happiness, and Well-Being; Shawn Achor; Currency; 2018

Barking Up the Wrong Tree: The Surprising Sicence Behind Why Everything You Know About Success is (Mostly) Wrong; Eric Barker; Harper One; 2017

The Luck Factor; Richard Wiseman; Arrow Books; 2004

HEALTH

Why We Sleep; Matthew Walker; Scribner; 2017

THE STATE OF THE WORLD

Utopia for Realists; Rutger Bregman; Little, Brown and Company; 2017

Bullshit Jobs; David Graeber; Simon & Schuster; 2018

Factfulness: Ten Reasons We're Wrong About the World—and Why Things Are Better Than You Think ; Hans Rosling, Anna Rosling Rönnlund & Ola Rosling; Flatiron Books; 2018

CRITICAL THINKING

Predictably Irrational: The Hidden Forces That Shape Our Decisions; Dan Ariely; Harper Perennial; 2008

Thinking, Fast and Slow; Daniel Kahneman; Farrar, Straus and Giroux; 2011

You Are Not So Smart; David McRaney; Gotham; 2011

The Paradox of Choice; Barry Schwartz; Harper Perennial; 2005

Situations Matter: Understanding How Context Transforms Your World; Sam Sommers; Riverhead; 2011

The Black Swan: The Impact of the Highly Improbable; Nassem Nicholas Taleb; Random House; 2007

INSPIRATIONAL

An Astronaut's Guide to Life on Earth: What Going to Space Taught Me About Ingenuity, Determination, and Being Prepared for Anything; Chris Hadfield; Back Bay Books; 2015

SOLIDARITY

Writing the Other; Nisi Shaw & Cynthia Ward; Aqueduct Press; 2005

ARTICLES

DOUBT

Impostor/Abuser: Power Dynamics in Publishing; Sarah Gailey; https://firesidefiction.com/impostor-abuser-power-dynamics-in-publishing

The Neil Story; Neil Gaiman; http://journal.neilgaiman.com/2017/05/the-neil-story-with-additional-footnote.html

Building the Story of Ourselves; Kameron Hurley; https://locusmag.com/2018/10/kameron-hurley-building-the-story-of-ourselves/

The Confidence Gap; Katty Kay and Claire Shipman; https://www.theatlantic.com/magazine/archive/2014/05/the-confidence-gap/359815/

Five Strategies for Dealing With Fear; Tara Mohr; https://www.taramohr.com/dealing-with-fear/5-strategies-for-dealing-with-fear/

Put Down the Self-Help Books. Resilience is Not a DIY Endeavor; Michael Ungar; https://www.theglobeandmail.

com/amp/opinion/article-put-down-the-self-help-books-resilience-is-not-a-diy-endeavour/

GRIEF AND HOPE

How Do We Go On?; Tabitha Carvan; https://science.anu.edu.au/news-events/opinion/how-do-we-go

10 Ways to 'Reach Out' When You're Struggling With Your Mental Health; Sam Dylan Finch; https://letsqueerthingsup.com/2018/03/03/10-ways-to-reach-out-when-youre-struggling-with-your-mental-health/

Silicon Valley Tech Workers are Using an Ancient Philosophy Designed for Greek Slaves as a Life Hack; Olivia Goldhill; https://qz.com/866030/stoicism-silicon-valley-tech-workers-are-reading-ryan-holiday-to-use-an-ancient-philosophy-as-a-life-hack/

The Uncanny Power of Greta Thunberg's Climate-Change Rhetoric; Sam Knight; https://www.newyorker.com/news/daily-comment/the-uncanny-power-of-greta-thunbergs-climate-change-rhetoric

N.K. Jemisin Is Trying to Keep the World From Ending; Joshua Rivera; https://www.gq.com/story/nk-jemisin-is-trying-to-keep-the-world-from-ending

SOLIDARITY

Stop Appropriating the Language That Explains My Condition; Naomi Chainey; https://www.smh.com.au/lifestyle/stop-appropriating-the-language-that-explains-my-condition-20160113-gm4whc.html

Speak Up & Stay Safe(r): A Guide to Protecting Yourself From Online Harassment; Feminist Frequency; https://onlinesafety.feministfrequency.com/en/

Hello! You Just Used the "Damned if You Do/Don't" Fallacy!; N. K. Jemisin; http://nkjemisin.com/2016/04/hello-you-just-used-the-damned-if-you-dodont-fallacy/

Cultural Appropriation in Books That Are Kinda Meh; Jeannette Ng; https://medium.com/@nettlefish/cultural-appropriation-in-books-that-are-kinda-meh-44c3491a2906

12 Fundamentals of Writing The Other (And the Self); Daniel Jose Older; https://www.buzzfeed.com/danieljoseolder/fundamentals-of-writing-the-other

Straight White Male: The Lowest Difficulty Setting There Is; John Scalzi; https://whatever.scalzi.com/2012/05/15/straight-white-male-the-lowest-difficulty-setting-there-is/

Being a Marginalized Author, Or What Do All These Knobs Do; Bogi Takács; http://www.bogireadstheworld.com/being-a-diverse-author-howto/

FRIENDS AND NEMESES

On the Importance of Community; S. L. Huang; https://absolutewrite.com/2018/11/28/on-the-importance-of-community/amp/

Debut Author Lessons: Status and Hierarchy Shifts; Mary Robinette Kowal; http://maryrobinettekowal.com/journal/debut-author-lessons-status-and-hierarchy-shifts/

Get Yourself a Nemesis; Taylor Lorenz; https://www.

theatlantic.com/health/archive/2019/03/how-choose-best-nemesis/585712/

FAILURE

Talking About Failure Is Crucial for Growth; Oset Babur; https://www.nytimes.com/2018/08/17/smarter-living/talking-about-failure-is-crucial-for-growth-heres-how-to-do-it-right.html

You Accomplished Something Great. So Now What?; A.C. Shilton; https://www.nytimes.com/2019/05/28/smarter-living/you-accomplished-something-great-so-now-what.html

Be Lucky - It's an Easy Skill to Learn; Richard Wiseman; https://www.telegraph.co.uk/technology/3304496/Be-lucky-its-an-easy-skill-to-learn.html

MAKING WORDS

Procrastination is Not Laziness; David Cain; https://thoughtcatalog.com/david-cain/2013/02/procrastination-is-not-laziness/

Five Scientific Ways to Build Habits That Stick; Gregory Ciotti; https://99u.adobe.com/articles/17123/5-scientific-ways-to-build-habits-that-stick

How Writing an 'Emotional To-Do List' Helped Me Push Past Procrastination; Kara Cutruzzula; https://advice.shinetext.com/articles/why-you-should-write-an-emotional-to-do-list/

The Pomodoro Technique; Aidan Doyle; https://www.sfwa.org/2015/05/the-pomodoro-technique/

Text Expansion Tools; Aidan Doyle; https://www.sfwa.org/2016/06/text-expansion-tools/

Bullet Journaling for Fiction Writers; Victoria Fry; https://www.somethingdelicious.co/2016/08/bullet-journal-writing-novel.html

GTD in 15 minutes - A Pragmatic Guide to Getting Things Done; Erlend Hamberg; https://hamberg.no/gtd/

How to Conquer Procrastination with 3 Self-Awareness Techniques; Niklas Göke; https://medium.com/s/the-complete-guide-to-beating-procrastination/how-to-conquer-procrastination-with-3-self-awareness-techniques-cc9546fe641d

WTF Is A Bullet Journal And Why Should You Start One? An Explainer; Rachel Wilkerson Miller & Ellie Sunakawa; https://www.buzzfeed.com/rachelwmiller/how-to-start-a-bullet-journal

How to Use Psychology to Solve the Procrastination Puzzle; Tim Pychyl; https://medium.com/s/the-complete-guide-to-beating-procrastination/how-to-use-psychology-to-solve-the-procrastination-puzzle-6e6a56cdd535

Why Procrastinators Procrastinate; Tim Urban; https://waitbutwhy.com/2013/10/why-procrastinators-procrastinate.html

THE LONG ROAD

How to Rest; Millie Baylis; https://www.killyourdarlings.
com.au/article/how-to-rest/

Is It Too Late to Follow My Dreams?; Roxane Gay;
https://www.nytimes.com/2017/12/30/opinion/sunday/
ask-roxane-is-it-too-late-to-follow-my-dreams.html

Conserving Spoons; Cynthia Kim; https://
musingsofanaspie.com/2014/10/15/conserving-spoons/

Writing is Terrible, Complaining About it Is Fine; Kelly
Link; https://lithub.com/kelly-links-advice-to-debut-
authors-writing-is-terrible-complaining-about-it-is-fine/

Spoon Theory; Christine Miserandino; https://
butyoudontlooksick.com/articles/written-by-christine/the-
spoon-theory/

TED (X) TALKS

The Danger of a Single Story; Chimamanda Ngozi
Adichie; https://www.ted.com/
talks/chimamanda_adichie_the_danger_of_a_single_story

The Power of Vulnerability; Brené Brown; https://www.
ted.com/talks/brene_brown_on_vulnerability

The Power of Introverts; Susan Cain; https://www.ted.
com/talks/susan_cain_the_power_of_introverts

The Power of Believing That You Can Improve; Carol
Dweck; https://www.ted.com/
talks/carol_dweck_the_power_of_believing_that_you_can
_improve

The Surprising Science of Happiness; Dan Gilbert;
https://www.ted.com/
talks/dan_gilbert_asks_why_are_we_happy

The Riddle of Experience vs Memory; Daniel Kahneman;
https://www.ted.com/
talks/daniel_kahneman_the_riddle_of_experience_vs_me
mory

The Best Stats You've Ever Seen; Hans Rosling; https://
www.ted.com/
talks/hans_rosling_shows_the_best_stats_you_ve_ever_see
n

The Art of Asking; Amanda Palmer; https://www.ted.
com/talks/amanda_palmer_the_art_of_asking

Inside the Mind of a Master Procrastinator; Tim Urban;
https://www.ted.com/
talks/tim_urban_inside_the_mind_of_a_master_procrastin
ator

THE AUTHOR

Aidan Doyle is an Australian writer, editor, and computer programmer. He is the co-editor of the anthology, *Sword and Sonnet*. His short stories have been published in places such as *Lightspeed*, *Strange Horizons* and *Fireside*. He is an Associate Editor at *PodCastle* and has been shortlisted for the *Aurealis*, *Ditmar*, and *XYZZY* awards. He has visited more than 100 countries and his experiences include teaching English in Japan, interviewing ninjas in Bolivia, and going ten-pin bowling in North Korea. http://www.aidandoyle.net @aidan_doyle

THE ILLUSTRATOR

Kathleen Jennings is an illustrator (and writer) based in Brisbane, Australia. She has created illustrations and cover art for many international authors and publishers, and her maps appear on the cover of Christopher Rowe's *Telling the Map* (Small Beer Press) and in Holly Black's *The Cruel Prince* and T*he Wicked King* (Little, Brown; forthcoming). She is a *Hugo* finalist, has three *World Fantasy Award* nominations, and has several *Ditmar Awards* to her name, and can be found online at kathleenjennings.com and tanaudel.wordpress.com.

ADDITIONAL ILLUSTRATIONS

Tom Gauld is a London-based cartoonist and illustrator, he makes weekly cartoons for *The Guardian* and *New Scientist*. He has created a number of comic books, including *Goliath* and *Mooncop*. His latest publication is *The Snooty Bookshop*.

Geert Weggen is a Dutch/Swedish internationally awarded photographer specializing in photographing red squirrels. His work is published in newspapers, books, calendars, on television and in magazines such as *National Geographic*. He just published a new book called *Weihnachten bei den Eichhörnchen* which is available in German bookstores. He has calendars published by Willowcreek and puzzles by Castorland. He organizes photo workshops in Sweden. Instagram/Facebook: geertweggen
https://geertweggen.com/

ACKNOWLEGMENTS

Thank you to Kathleen for all of her wonderful illustrations. Thank you to all of the contributors for their essays and images. Escape Artists, Codex, The Pandas, The Pastry Crew, Supernova, Alex Adsett, Bogi Takács, Tina Connolly, Kate Heartfield, E. Catherine Tobler, Eugenia Triantafyllou, Stephanie Charette, Elaine Cuyegkeng, Suzanne J. Willis, Sophie Yorkston, Alex Hong, Steve McLeod.

A big thank you to all of the Kickstarter backers.

Kim Allison, David Allkins, E. C. Ambrose, RM Ambrose, G. V. Anderson, PJ Anthony, Basket of Adorables, Jennifer B, Olivia Babb, Stewart C Baker, Alan Baxter, Dagmar Baumann, Kimberly Bea, Phillip Berrie, TJ Berry, Leonardo Bertinelli, Sofie Bird, Laura Blackwell, Kiana Brown, Lori Brown, Kristin Leydig Bryant, Clwedd Burns, Michael A. Burstein, Rebecca Burton, Kurt Busiek, Mike Cassella, Eliza Chan, Shenwei Chang, Stephanie Charette, Ann Chatham, Bright Chen, Anne L Chesterley, Kat Clay, Katharine Coldiron, Amanda Cook, Kelly J. Cooper, Vida Cruz, Elaine Cuyegkeng, Karl Dandenell, Sarah Dardick, David DeGraff, SB Divya, David Dyte, Iris E, Kate M. Eidam, Sean Elliott, James Henry Feeman, Kat Feete, Melissa Ferguson, Lisa Ferland, Elizabeth Fitzgerald, Lotta Fjelkegård, Patricia R. Fox, Anthony Francis, Di Francis, Marcia Franklin, Jason Franks, Fuchsi, M. E. Garber, Dorothy L. Gillmeister, GKahn, Abi Godsell, Samantha Goodfellow, Dave Graham, Jaq Greenspon, Renee Carter Hall, Erin M. Hartshorn, Sheryl R. Hayes, Shana Hausman, Tyler Hayes, Kate Heartfield, Sylvia Heike, Simone Heller, Amanda Helms, Miriah Hetherington, Kevin Hogan, Fermin Serena Hortas,

Jennifer Hudak, Crystal M. Huff, Liz Irving, Betsy J., Jim Johnson, Jess S Kautz, Juliet Kemp, Scott King, Benjamin C. Kinney, Kiraimu, Alisa Krasnostein, N.R. Lambert, Jon Lasser, Maya Lassiter, K. Bird lincoln, Camille Lofters, Kat Loot, Emma Lord, Stephanie Lorée, S. Qiouyi Lu, Alexandra McCallum, Ceallaigh S. MacCath-Moran, Beth Manalac, Dave Marshall, Premee Mohamed, Ashley R Morton, Mary Murphy, Cara Murray, Joel Naoum, Justin Nafziger, Sheryl Nantus, Consolata Ndungu, Thomas Negovan, David Nissen, NJGR, Sandra M. Odell, Aimee Ogden, Shauna O'Meara, Angela O'Rourke, Lisa Padol, KD Parker, Jim Parkin, Steven Paulsen, Laura Pearlman, Betsy Hanes Perry, Cynthia Porter, Tadgh (Lyon) Pound, Borys Pugacz-Muraszkiewicz, Jenny Rae Rappaport, Jane Rawson, Quinn Reynard, David M. Rheingold, Tansy Rayner Roberts, John Romkey, Frances Rowat, Anuj Rudhar, Merc Rustad, C. C. S. Ryan, Jill S, Victoria Sandbrook, Lorraine Schein, Lawrence M. Schoen, Bill Schulz and Kelley Hanahan-Schulz, Kimberley Sherry, Joe Slotnick, Cislyn Smith, Dave Smith, Maya Sonenberg, Cat Sparks, R. E. Stearns, R P Steeves, Maddie Stowe, Robert E. Stutts, Sweetkala, Kellan Szpara, Andrea Tatjana, Teddy, Lindsay Thomas, Davina Tijani, Leslie de la Torre, Eugenia Triantafyllou, Erika J Turnbull, Wayne Turner, Tyler, Craig Tyler, Emma Maree Urquhart, Cato Vandrare, Emma Varney, Dave Versace, Aljoša Vizovišek, KT Wagner, Lauren Wallace, Wren Wallis, Bonnie Warford, Simon Watts, What Cheer Writers Club, Laura Wilkinson, Sean Williams, Suzanne J. Willis, Jennifer Wilson, Filip Wiltgren, John Winkelman, Cliff Winnig, Erwin Wong, Sam Wood.

THE END OF THE BOOK ACTION PLAN

Reading advice is the easy part. Taking action is the critical part.

Choose a new daily habit. Find something you already do every day and start your new habit after it. Make your new habit as easy as possible to start. *After I finish my morning coffee, I will write for two minutes.*

Choose something you want to do less of. Make it twenty seconds harder to start. Remove social media apps from your phone. Put your TV remote in a different room.

Schedule times when you turn off notifications on your phone. Turn off autoplay on *Youtube* and streaming services.

Keep a gratitude journal.

Record how you spend your time for a week. Look for things you're doing that aren't useful and aren't making you happy.

Create an *Awesomeness Dossier*.

Try the Pomodoro technique.

Experiment with methods of tracking progress. An app, a calendar, stickers, gems in a bowl, a bullet journal.

Work out the three most important things you want to achieve with your writing.

Set SMART goals that will bring you closer to completing these dreams.

Choose a task you really want to do, but have always been putting off. Work out the next step. Decide on an implementation strategy. *I will go to the library after work on Wednesday and start writing the first chapter of my space opera.*

Find a writing accountability buddy.

Write something fun without the expectation that it will be published.

Schedule some play.

Join a new group.

Send a message to one of your favorite authors telling them how much you enjoyed their book.

Post online about how much you enjoyed a story one of your friends wrote.

Treat yourself kindly.

Help someone.

Schedule time to meet a friend you haven't seen in a while.

Give yourself permission to fail.

Try something you've never done before.